THE ABSOLUTELY WORST PLACES
TO LIVE IN AMERICA

DAVE GILMARTIN

THE ABSOLUTELY WORST PLACES TO LIVE IN AMERICA

THOMAS DUNNE BOOKS / ST. MARTIN'S GRIFFIN ☘ NEW YORK

THOMAS DUNNE BOOKS.
An imprint of St. Martin's Press.

www.thomasdunnebooks.com
www.stmartins.com

Library of Congress Cataloging-in-Publication Data
Gilmartin, Dave.
    The absolutely worst places to live in America / Dave
Gilmartin.—1st ed.
        p. cm.
ISBN-13: 978-0-312-35151-9
ISBN-10: 0-312-35151-8
    1. Quality of life—United States.   2. Cities and towns—
United States—Humor.   3. Cities and towns—United
States—Guidebooks.

HN60 .G55 2006
307.760973'090511—dc22

                                                        2006046439

First Edition: October 2006

10 9 8 7 6 5 4 3 2 1

For Amy, despite her location

Contents

Author's Note

The numbers cited in this book come from one of two sources. Population, Median Household Income, and Unemployment Percentages are from the United States Census Bureau's 2000 Census. Violent Crime Rate is from *Sperling's Best Places* Web site (www.bestplaces.net) and represents the number of combined cases of murder, nonnegligent manslaughter, forcible rape, robbery, and aggravated assault per 100,000 residents per year. The national average is 446.1.

THE *ABSOLUTELY WORST* PLACES
TO LIVE IN AMERICA

Introduction

As a former resident of Boston, Massachusetts, I'm painfully familiar with terrible places to live. I know, for example, what it is to get out of a movie at midnight only to discover the subway has already stopped running. I've had attempts to procure beer on Super Bowl Sunday thwarted by arcane blue laws. I've sat through a two hour poli-sci lecture at which Alec Baldwin popped in to stump for Ted Kennedy and flirt with the coeds. I've ridden a "subway" that smashed into a car. I've seen people travel across state lines to get a tattoo. I've ordered a cheesesteak at D'Angelo's only to have the fry cook shoot me a befuddled look, then say, "Oh, you mean a steak and cheese sandwich." I've attempted to decipher an accent for which the Rosetta Stone might have come in handy. I've sat directly behind a pillar at Fenway Park. I have, dear friends, witnessed a New York Giants absolute nail-biter of a late-December football game interrupted *late in the fourth quarter* in favor of the Patriots' opening kickoff. And this was the mid-nineties Patriots, keep in mind. And I'm not even a Giants fan. But these things don't happen in the real world.

Thing is, I now realize Boston probably isn't all that horrible. It didn't even make it into this book, which must account for something. Well, maybe. Truth be told, I didn't personally select the fifty horrifyingly dreadful places that did make the cut. This book is the result of a mostly democratic process, the product of six months spent asking people, "What's the worst place you've ever been?" Interested in gut reactions, and being quite lazy, I kept the question as broad as possible. It seemed a mistake to qualify my query, or to outline any specific methodology or standards re the results. One man's Paris is another man's Boston, after all. For me, it boils down to the people. What good is a nice café, after all, if it's filled with chain-smoking D.C. meatheads? But you might be into health care, or housing costs, or the school system, or the climate . . . whatever.

And so I left things vague, compiled the results, gave some consideration to geography (all the while fighting the urge to pick fifty from Florida alone), and voila: the following fifty armpits emerged. Are they truly the very worst towns in America? Let's just say that if you were to never step foot in any of them, well, you'd be all the better for it. Unless you're merely doing a bit of rubbernecking, of course, gawking at the terrible spectacle like it's a ten-car pileup of urban planning. That's always fun. But keep moving.

DG
Reno, 2005

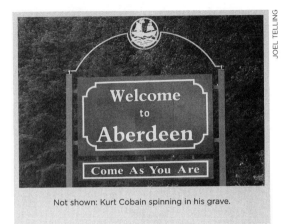

Not shown: Kurt Cobain spinning in his grave.

Aberdeen, WA

Gateway to the Olympic Peninsula
Birthplace of Grunge

Population: 16,461
Median Household Income: $30,683
Climate: Grey, rainy, and despondent
Ideal for: Loggers, Disaffected Youth
Cultural Highlights: Sulking, Moping, Rain, Boredom,
    Hero Worship, Cutting Down Lots and Lots of
    Trees, Abandoned Storefronts, Escaping to Seattle

An old logging and fishing village located on the southern edge of the Olympic Peninsula, Aberdeen combines all the classic disadvantages of waning industry with the newfangled horror of retail sprawl. Neither of which, however, has all that much to do with the city's notoriety. Nope, for bad as Aberdeen certainly is, its singularly shitty reputation stems from whatever source of inspiration it provided the young Kurt Cobain, semifavorite son/whipping boy/musical genius.

Though perhaps a tad obvious, the uniqueness of Aberdeen's pop culture contribution makes it impossible to ignore, as something must be said for a city so disagreeable that it managed to inspire a cultural revolution based almost entirely upon feelings of disaffection, alienation, malaise, and despair. That's really something. With the possible exception of Flint, Michigan, no U.S. city conjures images of utter dismay in the popular imagination as instantaneously as does Aberdeen.

Quotes

Aberdeen, Washington, has the highest rainfall of anywhere in the country. One hundred forty of 365 days of the year here have rain. The rest are probably fog.
—*from* The Bostoner, *by Andrew Buckley*

Aberdeen, Washington, is head and shoulders above most coastal areas in terms of pure, soul-crushing crappiness. Best known as the hometown of Kurt Cobain, it's easy to see how the seeds of suicidal dismay were sown. The beautiful waterfront is marked as a "Scenic View" despite being littered with the dead remains of ancient forest, courtesy of one of the big local logging operations. The true cultural beating heart of the area is Wal-Mart, with its parking lot full of trucks emblazoned with Bush-Cheney stickers despite the desperate economy. Elsewhere around town, churches with stained-glass windows and cute storefronts lie empty. The Salvation Army thrift store is a true *Dawn of the Dead* experience, with its distinct smell of mildew, old socks, and vast collection of shoulder-padded garments from the eighties. Some claim that the area is due for a renaissance. It will take a real visionary, that's for sure.

—*Melanie Sloan*

WISHFUL THINKING BY THE CHAMBER OF COMMERCE

"The most livable city in the state of Washington."

A GEOGRAPHICAL NOTE

Perhaps taking a cue from the weather or local disposition, Aberdeen is located in Grays Harbor

County and sits at the port of entry for Grays Harbor itself.

WIKIPEDIA SAYS . . .

"The city is made up almost entirely of a ghetto that extends into nearby Cosmopolis and Hoquiam, although there are some isolated areas of relative wealth. Aberdeen is sometimes called the 'Gateway to the Olympic Peninsula' or the 'Birthplace of Grunge'; however, locals generally term it 'Hicktown, U.S.A.'"

PERFECTLY ILLUSTRATIVE HEADLINES FROM *THE DAILY WORLD*

- "Man Claiming to Be Kurt Cobain Arrested"
- "Cobain Statue Long Overdo in Aberdeen"
- "A Brief Respite, Then More Rain"

Albuquerque's locally famous chain-link-fence-and-dirt district.

Albuquerque, NM

Population: 448,607
Median Household Income: $38,272
Violent Crime Rate: 1,250.7
Sports Teams Named for a *Simpsons* Episode: 1 (the minor-league baseball Isotopes)
Ideal for: Runaway Brides, Smelly White Hippies with Dreads, Aging New Agers, Mexican Gang Members and Their Offspring, *Outdoor* Magazine Subscribers, People with Incredibly Low Aspirations, Cholos and Cholas in Low Riders with Hydraulics

Cultural Highlights: Eating Mushrooms and Going to the Sandia Mountains, Drinking 40s, Hanging Out in Your Friend's Shack, Listening to the Grateful Dead and Phish, Shopping at the Co-op

Albuquerque is one of America's fastest growing cities, due mainly to the scores of confused and directionless neohippies who migrate southwest following high school graduation (or some approximation thereof). A melting pot of body odor, psychopharmaceuticals, Mexican food, strip clubs, jam bands, and trailer parks, the city is an ideal destination for anyone looking to relive the sixties or not challenge themselves in any tangible way (save for hiking).

Quotes

I was visiting Albuquerque with my girlfriend, who was looking into grad schools there. While walking around the downtown area in the middle of the afternoon, this hippie-looking guy with a camping backpack asked if he could purchase my girlfriend in exchange for some of his homemade necklaces and friendship bracelets. He could tell that I was not receptive to the idea, and said that he just needed to rent her for a couple of hours. He offered me my choice of jewelry, and when I denied him, he said, "Oh, man. You seemed like a cool guy.

—*Adam Mutterperl*

Albuquerque is a haven for New Age yuppie types, stinky hippies, college students, and the underclass. Highlights when I lived there were spotting cholos in their vintage low-riding cars with hydraulics, and eating freshly roasted peppers and the best flour tortillas. Lowlights were just about everything else. Rent was cheap, but your neighbors were likely meth or crackheads. Employment was hard to find and wages were crap. Aspirations were low. There was nothing to do there unless you were a tourist going to Old Town or a pothead hiker communing with nature. It sucked.

—*Theresa K.*

I lived in Albuquerque for seven months and if somebody offered me the chance to move back, I'd say "Hell, no." The people there are a perfect blend of Native Americans, Hispanics, Liberal Rednecks, and Crack Whores. In addition to the high drunk-driving and teen-pregnancy rates, it was virtually impossible to make any female friends, since practically every single girl in town has at least one kid and is only looking for someone to help raise it.

The layout is very odd, with every address having a NW, SW, NE, or SE after it, so you know where you are in relation to the "Big I" (the point where all the interstates intersect). Another major landmark is the Rio Grande, which looks more like a creek. It's anything but grand. Interstate 25 splits the city in two, with heavy gang and prostitution activity on the east side and all the hippies and Old Town (the touristy area) on the west. In Old Town, you can buy all the crappy turquoise jewelry and lava rocks your heart desires, plus park your car in a lot whose exorbitant prices are straight out of Beverly Hills.

A tip to anyone contemplating a move to Albuquerque: read up on the difference between red and green chilies before you go. If you can't readily determine the distinguishing characteristics of each, you'll be treated like the stupid gringo that you are.

—*Beth Dowell*

PERFECTLY ILLUSTRATIVE HEADLINES FROM *THE ALBUQUERQUE JOURNAL*

- "Defendant Wins 'Shroom Appeal"
- "Wolf Program Should Be Scrapped, Ranchers Say"
- "Ice Cream Man's Turn to Scream"
- "Wolf Supporters Speak Out"
- "Adult Bookstore Has Bernalillo Blushing"

WISHFUL THINKING BY THE CHAMBER OF COMMERCE

- "Nearly everyone who's ever been here has wonderful things to say about the city."
- "The best way to discover all the treasures our region has to offer is to experience them firsthand."
- "We believe that Albuquerque is a delightful place to live, work, and raise a family."

Boston college kids doing their best urban squalor impressions.

Allston, MA

The Student Ghetto

Population: 21,333
Median Household Income: $34,611
Climate: Grimy
Ideal For: Clueless College Students, Aging Rockers, Obnoxious BC Frat Guys, Slum Lords, Mods with Massachusetts Accents
Cultural Highlights: Faux Irish Pubs, Garbage, Vomiting in the Shrubbery, Drunken Brawling, Late Night/Early Morning Car Alarms, Smashing Beer Bottles, Brief Yet Intimate Encounters, Queuing for Overcrowded Bars, Making Last Call

Dominated by once-grand Victorian homes long since oversubdivided for use as student housing, Allston, Massachusetts is a melting pot of upper-middle-class white kids eager to experience a brief taste of rebellious semiurban squalor (provided the dilapidation does not preclude a wireless Internet connection). It is not unusual to see residents from as disparate origins as Boston University, Boston College, Harvard, MIT, Berklee, Northeastern, or even Smith dining together peacefully at one of the area's many ethnic eateries that exist solely to placate the whims of a populace collectively bummed out over not being in New York City.

Quotes

Allston sucks not because the people who live there are poor (quite the opposite), but because they have no respect for their surroundings.

—*Judi DeCicco*

It's hard to say which is worse: the rampant drug-fueled violent crime or the fact that each house seems to contain a terrible college rock band oblivious to its own lack of talent. To walk the streets of Allston, one must always be prepared to dodge either a switchblade or the spillover from a sweaty, male-heavy basement kegger. Allston's social scene possesses a certain grassroots lack of charm, with most activity centered around the crumbling, Mrs. Haversham-esque residential sector. Things have gotten so out of hand that the local police force must routinely thwart the activity of illegal basement speakeasies, thus draining their ability to fight real crime. Of course, the real culprit is Allston itself, a town so afraid of its own impulses as to legislate a preposterously early closing time for all bars and clubs (2:00 a.m. at the very latest). This, combined with the fact that the "subway" stops running at midnight, fuels the relentless feelings of restlessness and frustration commonly exhibited by Allston's already young and therefore naturally rowdy inhabitants.

—*Zane*

Kiss me where it smells, she said, so I took her to Allston.

—*David Foster Wallace*, Infinite Jest

 AUTHOR'S VIEW

The real problem with Allston, aside from the fact that it's part of Boston, is the transience of its population, which creates a double-edged drawback. First, since most people know they'll only be there for a few years, they feel free to treat everything around them like shit, the cumulative effect of which is staggering. Just look around—it's a dump. Second, and even more sinister, those who stay on after college are generally the most ineffectual and

Quotes

Baltimore has the STD and HIV rates of a third-world country.

—*Kyle Bernstein*

Let me tell you about Bawlimer. Bawlimer, Merryland, that is. It's good if you like crabs. It's bad if you have crabs. It thinks it's a cutting-edge city. They've spent millions on the Inner Harbor. I wonder, what is the Inner Harbor? It's like Disneyland in the middle of Afghanistan. Every once in a while people come out of their caves, only to find out that the number-one sport is not the Orioles, it's not the Ravens, it's dodging bullets.

Why, just the other day I had my purse snatched by a drive-by purse snatcher. He jumped out of a car in broad daylight and tore it right off my arm. I got the plates . . . and, of course, it was a stolen car.

On the other hand, we've got Johns Hopkins, the number-one medical institution in the world, plus Sheppard Pratt Hospital, one of the top-ten psychiatric facilities in the United States. So if you're sick or insane, Bawlimer is the place to be.

—*Micheline Birger*

Baltimore: the city where people get mugged in church.

—*Michael Tully*

Not only do park benches in Baltimore say "The Greatest City in America," but they're usually covered in pigeon shit and draped with at least one passed-out homeless person.

—*Ryan Brosa*

WISHFUL THINKING BY THE CHAMBER OF COMMERCE

"Baltimore: The Greatest City in America."

IT HAPPENED HERE!

On October 3, 1849, Edgar Allen Poe was discovered on the streets of Baltimore, "delirious and in great distress," according to reports from the scene. Four days later, the writer was dead, a demise popularly (though perhaps not quite accurately) attributed to the ill effects of drunkenness. Today, Poe is something of a favorite son, remembered both by the city's Baltimore Ravens football team and its endemic substance abuse issues.

Or you could just keep driving.

Barstow, CA

Crossroads of Opportunity

Population: 21,119
Median Household Income: $35,069
Violent Crime Rate: 740.3
Ideal for: Truckers, Tourists, Auto Mechanics, Tow Truck Drivers, Mexicans
Cultural Highlights: Refueling, Overpriced Auto Repair, Route 66, Fast Food, Kitsch, Cheap Housing

A glorified pit stop smack dab in the hot, dusty middle between Los Angeles and Las Vegas, Barstow appears from the distance like an oasis on the edge of the Mojave Desert, at least to those who are big fans of fast food and petrol. Perched at the intersection of several major highways, Barstow is a magnet for weary tourists and truckers, the result being that this former mining town, despite its still functioning strip of old, romantic Route 66, now seems largely indistinguishable from the rest of roadside, sprawl-ridden America. "We are a very truck-friendly town," says Jeanette Hayhurst, Barstow's economic development coordinator, as if that's a good thing. Throw in a slew of noisy railyards for good measure and Barstow reveals itself for what it is: a tolerable place to pass an hour or two.

Thing is, people actually live here, the one plus being that they've managed to discover what might be the only California town immune from the state's housing boom. Barstow's own official Web site boasts that, while the California median home price hovers around $522,930, houses are available locally for the low, low average price of $115,276. The reasons for this discrepancy aren't provided, though further perusal of the Web site (particularly the recreation and culture sections) offers some clues.

Quotes

Barstow brings back memories of air musky with the
scent of freshly baked trash and the constant waft of exhaust fumes. The local aesthetic consists of three varia-
tions on the color brown, which tends to inspire one to
keep driving. The only redeeming quality of Barstow is
the In-N-Out Burger.

—*Mark Harmon*

On my way back from a weekend in Las Vegas, my alter-
nator quit and I was forced to spend the night in Barstow
while my car was repaired at one of the town's many
shady repair shops. At night, Barstow is a ghost town. It's
dark. Desolate. The wind whips across the barren landscape, kicking up dust and dirt in every direction. I got a
room at a cheap motel, an establishment that seemed to
take its decorating cues from Norman Bates. My room
featured a cigarette-burned bed, a bathroom window
that would not close, and a cheap, ten-dollar doorknob
on the front door. Terrified someone might try to break
in, slit my throat, and rob me of my casino winnings, I
closed the bathroom door and placed a metal chair un-
derneath the doorknob to prevent anyone from entering
through the open window. Then I pushed the nightstand
against the front door. Satisfied my efforts would at least
slow an attacker, if not actually thwart him completely, I
crawled into bed and drifted off to sleep, only to be

awoken at five a.m. by the sounds of boxcar couplers smashing together at the rail.

—*Steve Cwik*

↗ A DISSENTING OPINION

Barstow is a wonderful place to live, work, and play, and melds the best of small-town qualities with an ideal location that provides quick access to big-city amenities. The sense of community is evident in events like the Mardi Gras parade, Route 66 Main Street USA car show, sand castle building contest, Miss Barstow competition, Fourth of July fireworks celebration, and numerous others. While many large cities struggle to retain the intimacy of the community and re-create the main-street feel of downtown, Barstow hasn't lost its small-town charm. In fact, it is the only city on Route 66 with its primary business district still located on the historic thoroughfare.

Located at the gateway to the Mojave National Preserve, Barstow offers a wide range of outdoor activities, including camping, hiking, and desert exploration (viewing seasonal wild flowers, geological points of interest, and petroglyphs). Other local natural attractions include Afton Canyon, Rainbow Basin, Black Canyon, and Inscription Canyon. In addition, Barstow is home to two very popular visitors' areas: Stoddard Valley OHV and the Calico Ghost Town. Stoddard Valley is one of the largest off-highway vehicle areas in the state and is a favorite for competitive off-road events. Calico Ghost Town, one of few remaining authentic Old West mining towns, is the most visited county park in San Bernardino County.

The city is a major transportation corridor, with more than 60 million people passing through each year. This many visitors not only brings significant economic vitality to the community but also provides shopping, restaurant, and other retail choices not seen in most small communities. Barstow Outlets and Tanger Outlets provide nearly a hundred outlet stores, and the community is fortunate to feature many fine restaurants as well as a limitless number of fast-food establishments.

The city's location, midway between Los Angeles and Las Vegas, and the vast highway network converging in Barstow, offers residents efficient access to the big-city amenities of Los Angeles, as well as the glitz and glamour of Las Vegas. The area is also an hour's drive to Big Bear Lake's year-round skiing, boating, and fishing. The economic pipeline offered by the highway systems has sparked interest from several Native American tribes and developers who are seeking to build destination resort casinos within the city. These establishments promise to bring all the excitement of a Las Vegas–style casino, including gaming, big-name entertainers and shows, hotels, restaurants, and RV parks, as well as thousands of jobs. These potential developments hold the promise of being the catalyst for major economic development for the city.

—John Rader, Public Information Officer for the City of Barstow

PERFECTLY ILLUSTRATIVE HEADLINES FROM THE *DESERT DISPATCH*

- "Feds Pledge Help with Traffic Here"
- "A Dry Heat"
- "Leonardo's Original Pizzeria Opens with Ribbon Cutting"
- "Up Close with Lizards and Snakes"
- "Freeway Crash Injures Three, Kills Horse"

JIM SIMONSON

Beloit, WI

Gateway to Wisconsin

Population: 35,775
Unemployment: 6%
Median Household Income: $36,414
Former Industry of Choice: Paper
Cultural Highlights: World's Largest Can of Chili,
Huffing Duster, Packers Games, Native American
Effigy Mounds, Frito-Lay

Declining industry helped transform this once thriving, blue-collar factory town into a dreary, fourth-rate college town where generic sprawl mingles with more specific horrors. There's a strip of fast-food chains, of course, and the requisite Wal-Mart/town center. But there's also a riverside park full of floating dead carp, as well as a rather eerie shopping mall where only the Wal-greens remains in business. In true Beloit fashion, this mall, though mostly empty for the past fifteen years, is nonetheless still outfitted with creepy, 1970s-vintage Santas and Frosties come Christmastime, as if all were well and normal.

Quotes

I think the most pathetic of all the pathetic Wisconsin towns can be found along the southern border of the state, in the rural wastelands of what we call "Lil' Ap-palachia." I grew up just outside the boring, rural, though only slightly pathetic town of Platteville, right across the border from Dubuque, Iowa. As you travel east from there, you get to bigger, equally crappy, yet not necessarily more colorful towns before hitting Be-loit, in the southeastern corner of the state. Beloit is not exactly in the heart of Lil' Appalachia, per se, but its cer-tainly on the periphery. It has one leg in the rust belt and the other in hillbilly central. Beloit was voted the Worst Town in America by *Forbes* for like a decade, which should tell you pretty much all you need to know.

These are some of the people you're likely to encounter in Beloit:

- **Chicago Detritus/FIBs** (Wisconsin slang for Fucking Illinois Bastards): People who've washed upstream from dismal blue-collar suburbs like Cicero or Berwyn. These displaced suburban scum wear short shorts, Cubs jackets, and Jheri Curls.
- **Bear Chest Beauties:** The Bear Chest is Beloit's only strip joint, but what Beloit lacks in volume, it makes up for in class. The Chest is populated by rundown waitresses with mad cellulite and neck tattoos. Never mind what the image of an actual bear's chest interposed with that of a stripper brings to mind.
- **Beloit College Wieners:** Clueless prep retards who cruise around town in Dad's old Volvo, mostly on the prowl for soft drugs and hard liquor. Otherwise, they just throw Frisbees at the trees.
- **Truck Stop Waitresses:** These ladies are not quite desperate enough to take a job at the Bear Chest, but they're really, really close.
- **Super Wal-Mart Slackjaws:** Beloit is home to the superest Super-Wal-Mart I have ever seen and is always packed with two-hundred-pound ladies squeezed into sweatpants.
- **Super Wal-Mart Mini-Slackjaws:** Smaller versions of the above, these tend to rove in packs. Mini-

Slackjaws bob for baubles in the crane machines and try to find enough quarters on the floor to buy a Sam's Choice soda.

- **Unemployed Former Mechanics:** The Beloit Corporation used to manufacture engine parts of some kind and is now a factory shell inhabiting a small island in the middle of the Rock River. The corporation went under in the early nineties, leaving thousands in Beloit unemployed. Unemployed Former Mechanics can be seen basking in the glow of a TV or at Booze, Burgers and Boogie, an old Beloit Corp. haunt.
- **Mexicano Cabelleros:** The embroidered cowboy shirt–wearing Cabelleros cruise the strip along SoBo (South Beloit) on the lookout for braless Beloit College coeds.

—*Mahrya Draheim*

WISHFUL THINKING BY THE CHAMBER OF COMMERCE
- "There's something special going on in Greater Beloit."
- "The choices in Greater Beloit are endless."
- "If you care about the arts, you'll feel right at home in the Greater Beloit area."

Birmingham, AL

The Pittsburgh of the South

Magic City

Population: 242,820
Unemployment: 6.3%
Median Household Income: $26,735
Violent Crime Rate: 1,118.5
Climate: All over the place: tornadoes, tons of rain,
   mild winters, random humidity
Former Industry of Choice: Steel

Ideal for: Reformed/Newly Sensitive Rednecks,
Bankers, Miss America, Runners, Drag Queens
Cultural Highlights: The Vulcan Statue, College
Football, Disowning the Past, Motor Sports, Golf

Abhorrent racial history aside, Birmingham is somewhat typical of post-industrial, third-rate American cities. Once so enamored of its steel industry as to embrace the slogan "Pittsburgh of the South," Birmingham somehow neglected to note that, for much of its own history, Pittsburgh, Pennsylvania, lamented being the Pittsburgh of the North. Today, biotechnology and banking are all the rage, and, while PR materials suggest a veritable heaven on earth, they should be taken with a healthy dose of salt. Yes, Birmingham may indeed be the cultural center of Alabama, but let's not get hysterical.

Quotes

You know you're in the South when they start offering you sweet tea, calling Pepsi "Coke," and calling everybody "Hon" in that stupid accent of theirs that makes them sound twenty IQ points lower than they actually are. In Birmingham, they'll offer sweet tea and if you say you wanted unsweetened they look confused and act like they didn't know it came that way. One of my friends from college was from Birmingham and she was a Southern belle, which basically means whore in training. She spent the four years looking for some rich guy to take care of all her needs (a double-wide and a beat up Cavalier) so she wouldn't have to do anything herself.

Thanks to the Birmingham steel industry (it's an old mill town), the city has more than its share of trains and pollution. When you drive through the South, it's blue skies and greenery. Then you get to Birmingham, where everything is grey and concrete. It's one big white-trash ghetto. Birmingham has to be the trailer capitol of the South. Seriously, the trailer-trash problem is out of control.

If you listen to Birmingham radio, don't expect much beside gospel and country. If you're lucky, you might be able to pick up sports or an oldies station on the AM band, but if you're driving through, bring plenty of CDs. This might also be the only city in America where you thank God for the existence of those normally depressing concrete highway walls, simply because they block your view of what lurks on the other side: Birmingham, Alabama.

—*Beth Dowell*

The people of Birmingham fall all over themselves trying to prove how not racist they are anymore. Their big rallying cry is, "Oh, that was so long ago," like it's ancient history or something. Well, the 1960s happened everywhere, yet I can't seem to recall black schoolchildren being firebombed in Portland, Oregon. So there must be something greater at work here than simply the era, you know? For Birmingham to distance itself from the past as it has is like saying Charles Manson's a great guy cause he hasn't killed anyone in a while. At what point does a city become irredeemable?

—Will

PERFECTLY ILLUSTRATIVE HEADLINES FROM THE *BIRMINGHAM POST-HERALD* AND THE *BIRMINGHAM NEWS*

- "South's Hispanics More Likely Are Male, Under-educated"
- "Society Wants 21st Century Marker Removed from Confederate Cemetery"

WISHFUL THINKING BY THE CHAMBER OF COMMERCE

- "Birmingham: Live the Dream."
- "Welcome to the Birmingham area! You'll find Birmingham to be one of America's best-kept secrets."

And you thought Boston had a crappy skyline.

Camden, NJ

Population: 79,904
Unemployment: 7.8%
Median Household Income: $23,421
Violent Crime Rate: 2,160.1
Mayors Convicted of Corruption During Past Twenty Years: 3 (see Notes on page 46)
Ideal for: Violent Criminals, State Prisoners, Frightened Undergrads, Touring Rock Bands, Marine Life, Lookouts, Uncomfortable Whites
Cultural Highlights: Danger, Blight, Despair, Violence, Drugs, Dead End Streets, Minor League Baseball, Tropical Fish

In 2004, Camden, New Jersey, finally defeated its archrival, Detroit, Michigan, for the title of Most Dangerous City in America, then took home top prize again in 2005. The distinction, based on Camden's strong showing in the areas of murder, rape, robbery, aggravated assault, burglary, and auto theft, was merely the latest accolade for the city once renowned as the home of Walt Whitman, RCA Victor, and the first drive-in movie theater. Today, visitors (i.e., those unfortunate enough to have become lost on their way to Philadelphia) might be surprised to learn that Camden was once a town where Enrico Caruso and Louis Armstrong came to record, where shipbuilding and other industry flourished, and which actually featured a dynamic middle class.

Camden's current city planners seem more interested in luring tourists to the waterfront than with improving the plight of its citizenry. How exactly a new stadium for the Camden Riversharks is supposed to benefit the scores of people mired in abject poverty several blocks to the east is anyone's guess. Similar thinking is also to blame for the parasitic and delusional relationship Camden imagines itself to share with Philadelphia, which looms across the Delaware River like a beacon in the night (despite being no great shakes itself). It is virtually impossible to read any literature concerning present-day Camden without being bombarded with references to the city's convenient proximity to Philadelphia, as if Camden were actually an outgrowth or annex of the

City of Brotherly Love, an outer borough, as it were. It goes without saying that the people of Philadelphia do not share this symbiotic worldview, and instead rightfully consider Camden as that shithole across the river, to be avoided at all costs.

Quotes

Camden is the scariest place in the whole country.

—Billy

I have lived in the suburbs surrounding the area my entire life, and at all costs I have avoided Camden. Recently, a friend got lost and ended up on the outskirts of the city. She stopped at a red light, a man approached, motioned for her to roll the window down, and told her that girls shouldn't stop at stop signs or traffic lights in that part of town.

—Audrey Wilz

Camden is now a shell of ever-ringing pay phones, flotillas of drug dealers on mopeds, notoriously bribe-hungry politicians, and flaming trash cans, sometimes all on the same corner. City developers seem to think that building a stadium for Bon Jovi concerts on the Delaware River will bring investment, but they seem to have forgotten that the Tweeter Center stands in the shadow of overcrowded Camden County Prison, smack in the middle of town.

—Daniel Nester

Camden is a city of abject, third-world poverty and desperation. The schools suck, the infrastructure is an embarrassment, the government is corrupt, and it is incredibly dangerous. Only those with zero social capital stay there. Anyone with any aspiration (which hasn't been drummed out of them from years of living among junkies, crazies, and criminals) gets out as soon as they can.

A tiny section has recently become sort of nice, with luxury apartments, a developed waterfront, even a restaurant or two. But if you step out from this tiny radius, you're still in violent, dangerous Camden. None of the new development has so much as attempted to address the rampant poverty. The schools still suck, the social services are bureaucratic, crime is rampant, and people continue to live in crumbling, delapidated row homes.

—Virginia

When you took office, there was no question that Camden was a city of great despair. But the people believed in you. Your own people believed you. You squandered your opportunities. The people of this city do have a problem, but they do not deserve to be the laughing-stock of urban America . . . you've made them that.

— *U.S. District Judge Joel A. Pisano, upon sentencing former mayor Milton Milan*

AUTHOR'S VIEW

While taking photographs for this book, I found my-self in the wrong part of many horrible towns, none of which compared to Camden. This was by far one of the most unsettling experiences of my life, one of the few times I've felt real, physical fear. Perhaps it was that I visited on a particularly dark and gloomy day, but it also might have been the legion of BMX-riding hooligans who trailed and surrounded my car through the ghetto, some shouting racial epithets, others offering drugs for sale. It looked like the French Quarter gone completely to seed, crossed with the general menace of *Escape from New York*. Do not go to Camden.

IT HAPPENED HERE!

On September 6, 1945, Howard Unruh became the country's first modern mass murderer, killing thirteen people (and wounding another thirteen) in just under twenty minutes during a rampage through East Camden.

Notes

1. Milton Milan: Sentenced to seven years in prison for taking mob payoffs, using city contractors to perform free work on his home, laundering money from a drug dealer, committing insurance fraud, using vehicles supplied for free by a towing contractor, and selling a stolen computer to an intern (www.courierpostonline.com/camden/m061601a.htm).
2. Angelo Errichetti: Sentenced to six years in prison and fined $40,000 for his involvement in Abscam, the fictional company set up by the FBI to lure public officials into accepting bribes (http://www.public-action.com/911/rescue/obq-abscam/).
3. Arnold Webster: Pleaded guilty to illegally paying himself $20,000 in school district funds after becoming mayor. He faced a potential sentence of sixteenth months in prison and $250,000 in fines, though only received six months of house arrest and was ordered to repay the $20,000 (http://www.dvrbs.com/CamdenPeople-ArnoldWebster.htm).

ASHLEY SMITH

Typical Campton landscaping.

Campton, KY

Population: 424
Median Household Income: $17,778
Climate: Bored
Wolfe County Police Officers: 4
Ideal for: Deer Hunters, Rock Climbers, Hermits, Mobile Home Salesmen, Pill Poppers, Oxycontin Dealers, Pot Farmers
Cultural Highlights: Moonshine, Marijuana, Cruising, High School Basketball, Clogging, Four Wheelin', Dynamite Fishing, Cock Fighting, Car Shows

Surrounded by beautiful country littered with the trash of generations, Campton is home to large numbers of the trailer-dwelling, welfare-collecting set for which the Appalachian region is famous. This one-square-mile town features a single traffic light, a run-down Dairy Queen, seven gas stations, and nearly as many liquor stores. Plagued by an apathetic attitude disguised as "doing it like daddy done," the town is communally void of ambition. Campton's lack of recreational options, combined with a surplus of drugs and alcohol, makes for quite a dreadful mix. Despite the presence of several dive bars, most locals prefer quaffing Bud Light in the privacy of their own truck.

Quotes

You know the people who only seem to emerge from the woods when the fair comes to town? Well, that's pretty much Campton year-round. And for some reason, it seems like all of them have the last name Dunn. It can be scary for a first-time visitor. You get this eerie feeling that at any moment a couple of good 'ol boys are going to jump out of their pickup and beat you with a banjo. For the most part, I'd say these fears are unfounded because, after all, Campton's been called the *Friendliest Town in the Appalachians*. But it's easy to be friendly when everyone is family.

With nothing else to do, the youth of Campton (and

this includes those aged sixty-five and under) are left to fill up on wine, hit a home-grown joint, and cruise the town. Each day at sunset, the town fills with low-rider S-10s, illegally tinted Camaros, souped-up Chevelles, and the occasional four-wheeler. This ritual, known locally as "cruising," consists of driving from one gas station at the end of town to the twenty-four-hour Shellmart at the other. This futile routine keeps the gas stations in business and may help explain the town's obsession with NASCAR.

Though shirts and shoes are quite optional in Campton, the dress code is worth mentioning. Each clique tends to still dress exactly as it did in high school. For the graduating (or dropouting) classes of the eighties, this means stonewashed jeans, mullets, and Metallica tees. The nineties' classes are still rocking big bangs and *Button Your Fly* shirts, while the younger groups are divided among flea-market faked FUBUs and imitation Tommy Hilfiger. Of course, all of these groups are linked together by a collective love for tight Levis and Lynyrd Skynyrd.

—*Danny*

I've lived in Campton for two years. I still remember the first time I had to vote. I followed the directions on my ballot and stood in line to cast my vote . . . in a barn. Which isn't so bad when you consider the fact that our city hall is in a double-wide.

—*Xeo*

I think by sagging their FUBUs and blasting 50 Cent from their Camaros, a lot of the teenagers in Campton are trying to make up for the fact that no black people live there. It's actually a pretty nice, culturally aware gesture.

—*Paul*

STEPHAN HACK

Carson City, NV

Population: 52,457
Median Household Income: $41,809
Named For: Christopher "Kit" Carson, frontiersman
Ideal for: Nature Lovers, Strip Mall Lovers
Cultural Highlights: Second-Rate Casinos, Red Meat,
   Sprawl, Keno, Neighbor Envy, Talking Houses,
   Camel Races, Consumable Frontier Spirit

Degenerate gamblers aside, Carson City is an ideal location for absolutely no one. Quite possibly the ugliest state capital in the United States (Trenton, New Jersey, included), the city is an overpriced and sprawling blight on its otherwise gorgeous surroundings. Nestled in a lovely mountain setting adjacent to the Sierra Nevada Range and located just north of breathtaking Lake Tahoe, Carson City appears like a zit on the chin of northern Nevada. Given the additional fact that Reno, one of the more desirable small cities in the country, beckons from thirty miles north, Carson City begs the question, "Why would anyone want to live *here*?" Well, most don't. Even those technically residing within the city limits, lured by the mountain lifestyle and temperate climate, go out of their way to avoid setting foot in the city proper. Though rumored to be on the rise, nothing short of another full-blown silver rush could make Carson City a desirable place to live, work, or play.

Quotes

If you've ever been to or seen a picture of Western Nevada Community College, you know exactly why Carson City sucks. Imagine this: a beautiful, snow-capped mountain range stretched out across the horizon in each direction. Then imagine a bunch of offensively ugly crap plopped down in the foreground: bland administrative structures, things that look like (and probably are) trailers, the kind of prefab housing preferred by quasi religious cults, all designed in an architectural style straight out of the midcentury Eastern Bloc. It's truly awful, the detritus of a tasteless society. Plus, not only is it repugnant, but it's just scattered about with an apparent disdain for community planning or intelligent thought. It's like taking the most beautiful forest in the world and setting it on fire. And if the ugliness doesn't kill you, that degree from Western Nevada Community College surely will.

—Jeff

I had to go to Carson City for a wedding once, and I can honestly say that nothing prepared me for how awful the place is. To make matters worse, I was in the wedding party and had to spend like four days in this shithole, trudging around to rehearsal dinners and a bunch of other crap. I know they're in love and everything, but visiting inlaws in Carson City is a steep price to pay for shacking up with some semiattractive girl. I spent most of the trip waiting for the groom to come to his senses, which he never did. It wasn't like I was expecting Vegas or anything, but come on. This place is an absolute dump. And I'm from New Jersey, so I know what I'm talking about. If I had to single out the worst aspect of Carson City, it would have to be that you get this sense that you're so close, yet so far from something that might be a hell of a lot better. It's like everyone there got together and said, "OK, how can we destroy this place?" Just completely frustrating.

—*Scott*

WISHFUL THINKING BY THE CHAMBER OF COMMERCE AND VISITOR CENTER

- "On the scale of capital cities, Carson City ranks among the smallest in the United States, but you wouldn't know it from all the action around town."
- "Nevada's capital offers more than you might think."

PUBLIC ALERT

Area subject to
mine subsidence
and
toxic gas emissions

Centralia, PA

Where Coal Is King

Population: Approximately 20

Unemployment: Difficult to say

Violent Crime Rate: N/A

Climate: Scalding

Zip Code: Revoked

Ideal for: Environmental Activists, Geologists,
Daytrippers, Off-Road Enthusiasts, Old-Timers,
Diehards, Holdouts

Cultural Highlights: Carbon Monoxide, Scavenging,
Danger

In the annals of crumbling, burned-out towns, none compare to the wasteland/roadtrip curio known as Centralia, Pennsylvania, where things are so bad that the ground is literally on fire. Once a bustling town of 1,100 people, fabled for its rich deposits of rare anthracite coal, Centralia has virtually vanished from the map, to the point that only a handful of defiant souls remain, surrounded by steaming ground, a few scattered homes (former row houses now supported on either side by steel H-beams), cracked roads, warning signs, and an eerily well-maintained hilltop cemetery. There is rumored to be a mayor, and thus some semblance of civilization, though exactly what quality of life or community exists within Centralia remains something of a mystery to those who stop by in order to gawk and snap photos.

Quotes

You know you're living in a bad town when your home can fall into a fiery sinkhole at any moment.
—*Dan I. Rad*

Centralia's fire is responsible for at least one positive feature: the ground has warmed to the point that certain flowers bloom unseasonably, creating a very ironic bit of beauty out of abject horribleness.
—*Ted Royer*

GREAT MOMENTS IN EMERGENCY LEGISLATION

Centralia's demise is as much a story of slowly burning underground mines as it is one of bureaucratic mismanagement, red tape, incompetence, and the disturbing reluctance of any official body to claim responsibility. Here then, without further ado, a condensed time line of the bungling miscalculations that helped condemn an entire town:

May 1962: The fire from trash being burned in a municipal dump moves into an adjacent mine tunnel. Local entities immediately begin haggling over whose problem it is.

July 1962: State officials visit and appraise the situation.

August 1962: Work begins excavating inflicted tunnels, the idea being to fill them with dirt.

October 1962: The project, incomplete, stalls due to lack of funding. It is later determined that the effort made the situation worse.

November 1962–August 1978: Various attempts are made to control and contain the fire, each of which fails, usually due to underfunding, poor decision making, and a general reluctance to take the issue seriously enough. Finally, the fire creeps to the edge of Centralia proper.

Fall 1979: Centralia residents begin to experience the fire's effects firsthand: smoky craters form in front lawns, steam rises from the ground, cellar walls are warm to the touch, snow refuses to stick, hot water runs from both taps. The government stands idly by.

1980: Twelve-year-old Todd Domboski plummets into a boiling, carbon monoxide sinkhole in his grandmother's yard. Though rescued by a cousin, the event makes national headlines, prompting the state to take half-hearted steps to protect the people of Centralia. In the interest of positive PR, gas detectors are installed and inspectors deployed.

1981: Temporary housing (mobile homes) is provided for citizens deemed to be inside the "fire zone," an inadequately tiny designation that leaves many in danger. Media coverage intensifies.

Late 1981: Initial buyout offers are made to a small percentage of suffering Centralians. That said offers seriously low-balled the recipients is an understatement. A rift spreads among the people of Centralia over the issue of relocation. The state's official position, that the fire will eventually burn itself out, remains unwavering. Thus, no further attempts to fight it are planned.

1981–1983: Finally accepting the fact that some compassion is owed the people of Centralia, state and local officials waste a couple of years bickering over the issue of from where this compassion should emanate.

November 1983: Congress appropriates $42 million for the relocation of Centralia. A decade or so of mismanaged efforts to remove the people of Centralia ensues. The period is marked by condemnation, manipulation, trickery, and a boondoggle of unnecessary rules, regulations, and procedures. Property sale is outlawed, removing any option other than the government's latest offer (which fluctuates over time).

1992: The government finally exercises its power of eminent domain.

1993: Route 61, the main artery into and out of Centralia, is closed indefinitely due to fire damage.

Present: The fire continues to burn and spread.

KENN KISER

Unfortunately, the fog isn't quite thick enough to completely obscure Cincinnati.

Cincinnati, OH

The Queen City
Porkopolis

Population: 331,285
Median Household Income: $29,493
Violent Crime Rate: 732.6
Worst Tourism Slogan Ever: "Downtown Cincinnati: Go to *Town*"
Subway: Unfinished and Abandoned
Ideal for: Midwesterners, Antiporn Activists, Noncreative Types, Major League Outfielders, Tafts

A charter member of Ohio's Holy Crap Trinity (along with fellow armpits Toledo and Cleveland), Cincinnati is the state's third-largest city and its leading producer of soap, cosmetics, urban sprawl, and racial tension. Located along the Ohio River in the southwest corner of the state, Cincinnati is often regarded as something of a crossroads between North and South, mostly in an effort to make it seem less bland. Unfortunately, what little excitement does exist often comes in the form of race riots and related activity (unless one considers the dismal meanderings of the Reds and Bengals "exciting"). In 2001, African American leaders called for a boycott of downtown Cincinnati. Prospective travelers looking for a good time are advised to follow suit.

Quotes

If you're looking for an ugly city with a serious race problem, try Cincinnati!

—Sara

Cincinnati makes me uncomfortable.

—Anonymous

As far as American destination spots go, Cincinnati fails to register. Who goes to Cincinnati for fun, or even on purpose? When's the last time you heard someone say, "We're honeymooning in Cincinnati"? It's practically impossible to be overshadowed by northern Kentucky, yet Cincinnati manages.

—*Danny R.*

WISHFUL THINKING BY THE CHAMBER OF COMMERCE

- "We invite you to take a look around and discover a region that's brimming with excitement, energy, and opportunities."
- "Ask relocating business owners why they chose Cincinnati and one answer predominates: the airport."

GREAT MOMENTS IN CINCINNATI HISTORY

- 1835: Cincinnati first receives the nickname "Porkopolis" in honor of its rich hog-packing tradition. Entire herds of swine roam the city streets.
- November 12, 1934: Charles Manson is born.
- 1977: Thirty-three-year-old Jerry Springer is elected mayor in the largest plurality in city history.

- September 1, 1978: *WKRP in Cincinnati* debuts on CBS.
- November 13, 1992: During civil court proceedings against the Cincinnati Reds baseball team, it is revealed that then owner Marge Schott referred to former Reds Eric Davis and Dave Parker as "million-dollar niggers." For good measure, Schott is also found to keep a swastika armband at home.

Now imagine the sound of nonstop jet planes overhead.

College Park, GA

Population: 20,382
Median Household Income: $30,846
Violent Crime Rate: 878.7
Colleges in College Park: Zero, unless one counts barber colleges or the Interactive College of Technology (most don't)
Ideal for: Prospective Rap Stars, Evangelists, Thugs, Winos, Gangbangers

Cultural Highlights: Crunk, Arrivals/Departures, Pawn Shops, Drugs, Gangbanging, Prostitution, Killin' Whitey, Cruising Around/Showing Off New Twenty-four-Inch Spinners

Ted Turner aside, everyone knows Atlanta sucks (lest there be any doubt, real cities don't refer to themselves as "Hotlanta"). Yet even this pseudo McCity, preposterous as it may be, is a Shangri-La compared to its neighbor, a realm of crime, razed buildings, and televangelists currently in the midst of a transition from community to runway. This is College Park: misnamed, frightening, and above all, undesirable.

Quotes

College Park, Georgia, is a super-crappy suburb of Atlanta. It's a ghetto on the south side of the city that is dominated by the monstrous, obnoxiously large Atlanta airport. Much of the town (including the house where I lived) has been torn down to expand the airport, a project that has never been completed, even though the demolition occurred years ago. So, about half of College Park is a creepy ghost town. The other half is pure nightmarish southern ghetto. Those unfortunate enough to live there are constantly bombarded by the loud noise of planes landing at the airport. It's hard to beat the annexation of the airport and the machinations of televangelist greed-mongers like Creflo Dollar to make a town basically unlivable and worthy of the title "Worst City in America." No one in College Park wants to be there.

When I was in fifth or sixth grade (and one of the only white kids in our part of the city), our school had a party at a local skating rink, and the mascot of this place was a guy dressed up as a pig who would skate around the rink. At this party, the DJ jokingly asked the kids, "Hey! Which one of you kids can catch the pig?" Well, a gang of kids not only caught the pig, but proceeded to beat the shit out of him. They tore the pig's head off, revealing a scared high school kid pleading for his life. Not only was no attempt made by the grownups in charge to break up this melee, but the roller-rink employees seemed rather amused by the whole spectacle.

Thing is, this wasn't an isolated event from my time there. I've lived in some violent, shithole towns and have spent time in quite a few large cities, and I've never seen more violence occur in any place I've been than I did while growing up in College Park. It saddens me a bit because I'm a Southerner who definitely misses living in the region of my birth. My problem with College Park was and is that it's a Southern town that makes absolutely no attempt at Southern charm. It's totally transparent and has no personality of its own; it's a ghetto like every ghetto. If it weren't for the fact that half of the city has been demolished to make room for airport runways that haven't yet been built, College Park could be East St. Louis, or Watts, or Gary, Indiana, or the scary city in any metropolitan area that no sane white person wants to enter. It's a shame to find such a place in the South, since, if anything, that area is supposed to be the nation's pinnacle of hospitality. You'd never form that conclusion wandering the streets of College Park, or seeing how people interact there, or sampling the yucky brand of scary Christian television that is produced there. Beside the fact that a couple of rappers and boxers came from there (and subsequently got the hell out once they could afford to), there's really nothing nice I could say about College Park.

—*Brian Dowell*

Though College Park is starting to see some redevelopment on the outskirts, it's still a very, very rough neighborhood, certainly not a place you want to be after dark. College Park, like many of the southside areas in Atlanta, is a very run-down, old, industrial sector . . . not very pretty. Even the hookers on Metropolitan Avenue (not College Park proper, but in the adjacent Hartsfield-Jackson Airport area) look old, worn-out, and dangerous. The airport area is a very low-rent, high-drug area, one that would rival similar areas in other major cities.

—*Alan Stanwick*

DEVLIN DARK

Cranston, RI

Dum Vigilo Curo (While I Watch I Care)

Population: 79,269
Median Household Income: $44,108
Middling Pop Culture Contribution: Elisabeth Filarski
Ideal for: White Trash, Mallrats, Mafia Wannabes, Ultra
  Guidos, Old-School Metal Heads, Paper Clip
  Company Employees

Cultural Highlights: The Sprague Mansion, I-95, Tight Jeans, Arson, The Olive Garden, The Ice Rink, Mall Shopping, The Unusually Depressing Cranston Historical District

Cranston, Rhode Island, seems to exist for the sole purpose of refuting every single positive characteristic of nearby Providence, its vastly superior neighbor to the north. Providence is progressive, artistic, and surprisingly metropolitan. It boasts a charming waterfront, great restaurants, even an Ivy League institution. Cranston boasts none of these things. If Providence is a quirky cross between Brooklyn and New England, Cranston is a dispiriting cross between North Jersey and a Ratt music video.

Though the cities are separated by a scant five miles, to travel from one to the other is to experience a cultural shift similar to that which might result after climbing into a time machine and setting the controls for twenty years prior. Visiting Cranston is like waking up inside a Chess King outlet store circa 1986. It's unsettling, disorienting, and garish, yet all in an uncomfortably familiar and personally shameful way. Cranston's like cultural déjà vu, the difference being that you really *have* been here before; you've just tried your best to forget.

Quotes

Cranston, Rhode Island, is hideously ugly, depressing to the point of surrealism, and one of the last great hair-mousse holdouts on the Eastern Seaboard. Sure, they've got urban sprawl and an astonishing absence of anything even remotely culturally appealing—but the worst thing about "Rhode Island's third largest city" is the indecipherable accent. You can't imagine the ways in which Cranstonites mangle the English language. Honestly, they all sound moderately to severely retarded. People from Providence can't even understand the dialect. Cranston folks say things like "take out the goobage."

—*Adam Mutterperl*

Aqua Net and nail salons will never go out of business as long as Cranston exists. Big hair and nails are still in style there, like it's New Jersey circa 1987 or something. And spandex will probably always be able to find a home in Cranston. Tammie Faye Baker could make a fortune with a beauty shop there, teaching customers how to properly apply makeup with a trowel.

—*Pam Oakman*

PERFECTLY ILLUSTRATIVE "TOP STORIES" FROM WJAR TV NEWS

- "Owner Waits by Open Cage Hoping Parrot Will Return"
- "School Janitor Arrested for Allegedly Having Drugs at Work"
- "Man Who Runs Model Agency Charged with Assaulting Clients"
- "Local Dog Track Desperate for More Money"

Detroit's somewhat subpar version of Grand Central Station.

Detroit, MI

Motor City
Motown
Murder City
D-Town; The D (for hip-hop use only)

Population: 951,270
Unemployment: 7.8%
Median Household Income: $29,526
Violent Crime Rate: 2,253.9
Climate: 75 sunny days per year

Positive Feature: The Former NBA Champion Detroit Pistons

Last Five People You'd Want to Encounter in a Dark Alley: The Former NBA Champion Detroit Pistons

Ideal for: Crack Whores (In Winter Coats, G-strings and Tennis Shoes), Muslims, the Homeless, the Toothless, Chronic Gamblers, Murderers, Innocent Bystanders, Starving Hip-Hop Artists, Fifteen-Year-Olds with Guns, Corrupt Police, Corrupt Mayors, Pissed-Off Auto Workers

Cultural Highlights: 4:00 a.m. White Castle Burgers, Traffic, Never-Ending Road Construction, STD-Infested Hip-Hop Clubs and Techno Raves, Cars, Car Companies, Bullets, Condemned Buildings

Ah, Detroit, birthplace of the American automobile industry, the Motown Sound, white flight, and urban sprawl. A crumbling, stagnated inner city surrounded by miles and miles of mostly middle-class suburbs (filled with people who rarely, if ever, actually set foot downtown), Detroit serves as a helpful reminder of what not to do with a big city. A teetering husk of its former industrialized, mighty self, Detroit is a city of ruins, littered with abandoned buildings and the ghostlike remnants of vanished neighborhoods. Throw in some racial segregation straight out of old-school South Africa and a violent crime rate nearly double the national average, and a rather dismal picture begins to emerge. Things are so bad that the word "Detroit" has come to symbolize urban danger and decay to much of the country. It is practically impossible to speak of terrible American cities without beginning (and ending) with Detroit.

Quotes

When you cross the city line coming in from the suburbs, you'll swear you made a wrong turn into Fallujah. (Tell locals you just drove downtown and watch their eyes go wide, like you're out of your mind for even considering such a thing.) The stores suddenly don't have windows (they aren't broken, the buildings are just made like blockhouses), trees and grass disappear, and the city can't seem to demolish crack houses faster than they multiply. Abandoned buildings abound. The city airport is now closed again. It's not as depressing as the abandoned Cadillac factory, though, since some private planes still use it. The weirdest thing about Detroit is the creep of urban decay into suburbia. Once-nice neighborhoods have turned over. They still look okay from a distance, until you notice the broken-down cars in the driveways, the trash floating around, the houses drifting slowly into disrepair. Weeds rule the lawn, graffiti pops up, home repairs are begun but never finished.

And good luck getting your foreign car serviced or locating a gym. This is Fatland, USA. You can't walk anywhere, and there's no public transportation to speak of, unless you count the laughable "People Mover." Maybe GM convinced the city to kill the streetcar service years ago. To be fair, there is supposedly a bus, but I've never actually seen it. There are bus stops, though.

—*Christopher Cotter*

Picture the GE building surrounded by three or four square blocks of a somewhat normal city. Once outside that radius, you step into the world of Robocop, which was actually filmed in Detroit because it already had the rundown, abandoned buildings and slum streets that fit the movie's theme. Hollywood didn't even have to build a set for the movie; they just flew to Detroit.

—*Nick Lopes*

The city planners were so worried that the dumb-ass Detroit morons would get lost, they had to name the streets based on how far from the city center they are . . . hence 6 Mile, 7 Mile, 8 Mile, and so on. Within the first two weeks I was there, two people working on my project watched as a man got slashed in the face outside Target. Then the Blockbuster next to our grocery store was robbed at gunpoint. Put it this way: from then on we voluntarily drove twenty miles for groceries.

—*Melissa Anderson*

If you're after a place that appears strikingly similar to Lucifer's residence, Detroit is what you're looking for. When you have to watch fifteen minutes of local news just to get past the day's murders, you know the city blows. Usually, we'll get a newscast that goes something like this: "Eight-year-old child shot on the east side this afternoon (who the hell shoots people in the afternoon, by the way?). . . . One-year-old falls out of window after parents got high and forgot about him. . . . Seventeen-year-old is the prime suspect in a double murder on 8 Mile last night. . . . An elderly woman was killed in a hit-and-run at 4 p.m. this afternoon, suspect still at large. . . . Two people were shot, but thankfully are only in critical condition at this time. . . . Mayor Kwame Kilpatrick allegedly had another crazy party at his mansion this weekend. . . . Oh, and by the way, thirty people were killed in a car bombing in Iraq."

If you really want to know what Detroit is all about, check out Mayor Kilpatrick. He's been accused of holding orgies in his mansion (no joke) and for spending public money on his wife's SUV, plus he responded to a misconduct investigation by firing the officer in charge. No wonder he's been named one of the worst big city mayors in the country.

—*Brandon Bera*

ONLY IN DETROIT

Detroit is said to be home to the Nain Rouge, a mythical red dwarf who attacks people and brings bad luck to the city. Judging by appearances, he's been quite thorough.

 A CATALOGUE OF DUBIOUS ACHIEVEMENT

Detroit is a magnet for plaudits, titles, and similar decoration. In fact, it's practically impossible to fully account for the multitude of honors bequeathed upon this fair city. The following represents a mere sampling of recent accolades.

- America's Fattest City, 2004 (*Men's Fitness* magazine)
- STD Capital of the United States, 2004 (*Men's Health* magazine)
- Most Rapidly Shrinking Population, Large City Division (Southeast Michigan Council of Governments)
- Runner-up, Most Depressed City, 2005 (*Men's Health* magazine)
- Top Three Worst Big City Mayors (Kwame Kilpatrick), 2005 (*Time* magazine)

Portly Pedro y plenty of parking.

Dillon, SC

Population: 6,316
Median Household Income: $25,267
Climate: Quite sunny and pleasant, actually
Ideal for: Honeymooners on a Serious Budget,
Campers, Weary Travelers, Easily Amused Small
Children, Ethnic Stereotypes
Cultural Highlights: Cheaply Made T-shirts, Mini Golf,
A Giant Sombrero Tower, Arcade Games,
Fireworks, Novelty Souvenirs, Indigestion

It's usually a bad sign when your town rests along Interstate 95, quite possibly the country's most annoying highway. Known for its never-ending construction, haphazard traffic patterns, and utter lack of interesting scenery, I-95's unrelenting drudgery is a main reason East Coasters become wide-eyed and spiritual when driving cross country.

Dillon at least tries to alleviate the monotony. The town is trumpeted from miles away, its very existence granted more ad space than a Hollywood summer blockbuster. Why all the fuss? Because Dillon, erstwhile insignificant small town, is home to one of the country's great tourist traps, the Hispanic-themed wonderland South of the Border, craptastic bargain theme park nonpareil.

Quotes

My family used to stop at South of the Border on our way to Florida each year. Until, that is, I had a fateful run-in with a burrito that has since become something of a family legend. Let's just say that in addition to fireworks stores and crappy motels, Pedro fortunately provides plenty of restrooms.

—*Jerry*

I'm from an actual border town—Laredo, Texas—and let me tell you, border towns are unbelievably horrible places to live. You really can not begin to imagine how shitty they are until you've lived in one: crime, filth, constant skirmishes and poor amenities are all border-town mainstays. The first time I saw Dillon's famed South of the Border, it blew my mind. A theme-park version of the worst place in the country is just an incredible concept. Actually, it got me thinking about the ideas that must have come in second: Backwoods Appalachian World, Ethiopian Famine Land, Skid Row Adventure, Siberian Gulag Kingdom, Pol Pot's Year One Fantasy Isle, Six Flags' Bataan Death March Safari . . . seriously, it's almost on that level.

—*John*

Pedro might be the most offensive ethnic caricature since Steppin' Fetchit. The ACLU must be too busy protecting the rights of subway bombers to do something about this place.

—*Patrick*

AUTHOR'S VIEW

South of the Border's famous series of amusing billboards really is the best thing about a road trip to Florida, Florida included.

MEXICANS ARE FUNNY: A SHORT
COMPENDIUM OF ETHNIC PUNS

The following choice tidbits are prominently featured, verbatim, on Dillon's own South of the Border Web site. Andale!

- "Pedro VER' GLAD YOU COME!! Pedro got 112 meelion amigos, who stay weeth heem, opp teel now all satisfy come back, send frans . . ."

- "Pedro sez: '*eef you follow Pedro's signz, ze treep seem MOCH shorter!*'"

- "Bring along the whole family for fun at Pedroland Park! *Pedro has sometheeng for every juan.*"

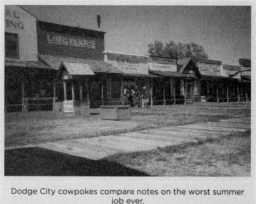

Dodge City cowpokes compare notes on the worst summer job ever.

Dodge City, KS

Queen of the Cowtowns
The Cowboy Capital

Population: 25,176
Median Household Income: $37,156
Local Buffalo Killed in Six Years: 1,500,000
Ideal for: *Gunsmoke* Aficionados, the Easily Amused,
 Ranch Hands, Cattle
Cultural Highlights: Gun Fight Reenactments, Church,
 the Rodeo, Beef, Ten Gallon Hats, Spurs

Dodge City trades on its Wild West roots to the extent that it's easy to wonder if anything's happened there since. From the looks of things, not really. Yeah, there's a public swimming pool, and they've got cars and running water and laws now, but the overall effect is of a town so fixated on its past as to resemble a tourist-friendly recreation of itself. It's like Colonial Williamsburg, but with people actually living in it. Once the gateway to the Santa Fe Trail, the precinct of Wyatt Earp, the very epitome, in many ways, of the American West, Dodge City is now just another kitschy roadside attraction, and a cut-rate one at that. Get the hell out of Dodge, indeed.

Quotes

Dodge City is the most dismal, upsettingly gross town. When people say the phrase, "Get the hell out of Dodge," it's for a reason! It smells like shit . . . literally. Cows and their poo is so popular in the town that they've set up a scenic overlook of the huge expansion of cows—many days you can just see the methane hover above. It's the most disturbing overlook with nothing scenic about it!

—*Chrissy Heikkila*

—It's the very street Wyatt Earp used to keep law and order on.

—It seems kind of dirty and touristy.

—Oh, Ellen, the Old West was dirty.

            —*from* National Lampoon's Vacation

WISHFUL THINKING BY THE CHAMBER OF COMMERCE

- "Dodge City . . . feel the excitement."
- "Dodge City is known world wide for tourism and the famous Boot Hill Museum."

DODGE CITY FROM THE COUCH

For those who can't make the trip, Dodge City's longhorn-drivin', whisky-drinkin', gunslingin' heyday can be experienced from the comfort of your own living room, without splurging for overpriced attractions or interacting with any pesky Kansans. What's more, since most of the following top off at under two hours, return to the real world is both simple and imminent. Check out one or two of these classics, then go to Disney World like a normal person.

- *Dodge City* (1939)—starring Errol Flynn and Olivia de Havilland
- *Gunsmoke*—television series, starring James Arness, Amanda Blake, Dennis Weaver, etc.

- *The Gunfight at Dodge City* (1959)—starring Joel McCrea and Julie Adams
- *A Big Hand for the Little Lady* (1966)—starring Henry Fonda, Joanne Woodward, and Jason Robards
- *King of Dodge City* (1941)—starring Bill Elliott and Tex Ritter

THINGS TO DO IN DODGE CITY IF YOU MUST

If a trip to Dodge City proves truly unavoidable, savvy and particularly optimistic visitors may manage to reasonably amuse themselves at one or more of the following "attractions."

- **Coronado Cross:** What's more fun than a thirty-eight-foot-tall cross standing out in the middle of nowhere? Why, a thirty-eight-foot-tall cross marking the spot where one Francisco Vasques de Coronado *may* have crossed the Arkansas River while searching for the Lost City of Gold, of course.
- **Gunfighter's Wax Museum:** As if the live re-enactments weren't waxlike enough, this museum features faithful recreations of all your favorite romanticized criminals, from Jesse James to Billy the Kid.
- **The Kansas Teacher's Hall of Fame:** A cross between Cooperstown and fifth-period Latin, the Hall of Fame is a destination spot for education

junkies everywhere. Thrill to an in-depth exploration of the flip-top desk, then stop off at the gift
shop for a T-shirt bearing the likenesses of the
state's most famous school marms. For kids, the
Eraser Clapping Simu-Tron is a real treat.

MONICA TERESA ORTIZ

Quite possibly the ugliest vista in the continental United States (with apologies to Newark, NJ).

El Paso, TX

Population: 563,662
Median Household Income: $32,124
Violent Crime Rate: 686
Climate: A Dry Heat
Former Industry of Choice: Copper
Ideal for: Day Laborers, The Military, Border Police, Hispanics
Cultural Highlights: Silver Jewelry, Leather, Curios, Margaritas, Tacos, Ciudad Juarez, NAFTA, Low-Cost Labor, Mountain Time

They say that things get worse the farther south you go. Well, El Paso is close to the end of the line. Large, isolated, and crappy in ways that only a border town can be, El Paso takes two cultures and mashes 'em into a hybrid of which neither can be terribly proud. Nestled, or mired, in the extreme southwest corner of the state, El Paso is sort of like Los Angeles without the film industry, which is to say without the glitz, culture, amenities, relevance, or excitement. Famous for its enchiladas, low-cost labor, and abhorrent hygiene, El Paso is made even less attractive by its near desperate economy (affected, as is it, by such preposterous factors as the fluctuation of the *peso*), violent crime, and lack of physical fitness.

Quotes

El Paso makes you want to triple-lock your motel room door for fear of a Mexican revolution, or just a basehead looking for a hamburger.

—*Scott Moe*

El Paso sucks. The roads and the buildings are all the same depressing color, and everything is all spread out and all over the place, leaving a ton of random, dry, dusty stretches of open land. And, of course, Mexico is literally a barb-wire fence away—how inviting! A million of the dirtiest, poorest-looking slums in the world are clearly visible through the fence; they're all bunched up on top of one another, and sit on a hill. So it's impossible to escape the sight of Mexico in all its poverty-stricken glory. Oh, and I might add that there's no cell phone service. So in theory one could wander over to the other side of the fence and disappear forever. Sounds like paradise, doesn't it? The words to keep in mind when thinking about a trip to El Paso are "brown" and "gross."

—*Lindsay Key*

PERFECTLY ILLUSTRATIVE HEADLINES FROM THE *EL PASO TIMES*

- "El Paso Teen Held in Juarez Jail Ages, Matures"
- "Migrants Caught, Deported Just Keep Trying"
- "Heroin, Meth Seizures Skyrocket"
- "Hurt Cowboy Crawls Home Three Miles"

WISHFUL THINKING BY THE CHAMBER OF COMMERCE

- "El Paso is a jewel in the desert."

A winter wonderland.

Fairbanks, AK

Golden Heart City

Population: 30,224
Unemployment: 6.2%
Median Household Income: $40,577
Violent Crime Rate: 1,074.6
Climate: Cold and dark/blindingly bright
Ideal for: Drunken Natives, Gun Loving Libertarians, Back-to-Nature Commune-Failed Hippies, Fundamentalists, Cabin-Fever-Addled GIs

Cultural Highlights: Dog Sled Races, Indoor Tanning, Strip Clubs, Bars, Drinking, Drugs, Drinking, Hunting, Drinking, Shooting People

Take the worst place you've ever been, then subtract the sun. That's Fairbanks, where each winter sunlight disappears almost completely for a convenient three-month stretch, during which time the average temperature hovers around a lovely fifteen below. Residents grope their way through the dark season against the dim backdrop of the northern lights and amuse themselves by drinking large quantities of alcohol, going insane, and doing fun stuff like filling a mug with hot water, walking outside, and tossing the water into the air to see if it evaporates before hitting the ground (an activity that seems really cool and interesting exactly twice).

When summer finally arrives (and with it days of twenty-four-hour sunlight), the people of Fairbanks spill out into the streets, wide-eyed, jubilant, and a bit dazed, like zombies risen from the grave. There is much festive rejoicing, more drinking, and baseball games played under the midnight sun (just because it's possible). The glowing orb provides such relief and happiness that it can take several weeks for depression to return, this time inspired by the sight of what has been illuminated: bland, flat Fairbanks, Alaska.

Quotes

First, the architecture: It's *horrible*. I can't adequately convey to you the awfulness of it. It's like fifties stone brutalist architecture, left out in the junk yard to decay.

Second, the winter: twenty hours of darkness with forty-below weather, plus ice fog thrown in for good measure. You can't see ten feet in front of your nose. It's like being on the moon, but worse.

And third: the substance abuse. I mean, there is *nothing* else to do there all winter. People just drink and smoke and inject away their cabin fever, because it's not like getting outside is going to make you feel any better.

—*Rick Webb*

THINGS TO DO

Fairbanks offers world-class entertainment, at least by Arctic Circle standards. There are myriad social options, so visitors should not limit themselves to quaffing cheap beer in dark bars. The city's wealth of cultural choices are highlighted by the following groups and organizations:

- Arctic Dreams Sled Dog Adventures
- Sun Dog Express Dog Sled Tours
- Chena Dog Sled Adventures
- Chugach Express Dog Sled Tours
- Alaska Dog Mushers Association

NORTHERNMOST SPRAWL

Fairbanks's official Web site boasts, with some pride, that the city is home to the country's northernmost McDonald's, Wendy's, Pizza Hut, Sears, Taco Bell, and Sam's Club. As if that weren't impressive enough, Fairbanks also features the northernmost dirt racetrack, the Mitchell Raceway.

PERFECTLY ILLUSTRATIVE HEADLINES FROM THE *FAIRBANKS DAILY NEWS-MINER*

- "Border Fire Draws Attention"
- "Cold Kills Local Man"
- "Children Asked to Name Police Dog"
- "Moose Encounters Increase as Days Grow Colder, Darker"
- "Young People Want Not Boring Stuff"

A scene from Fitchburg's crumbling factory/crack house quarter.

Fitchburg, MA

The City by the River

Population: 39,102
Median Household Income: $37,004
Violent Crime Rate: 1,206.7
Former Industry of Choice: Paper
Ideal for: Greasy Caucasians, Gang Members, Guidos, Mediocre Students Forced to Fall Back on Fitchburg State College, Drunken Frat Boys, Vomiting Sorority Girls, Slum Lords, Coke Heads, Pregnant Moms Who Beat Their Kids at the Grocery

Selecting the worst town in Massachusetts is a bit like singling out your least favorite Sugar Ray track. Like New Jersey, Pennsylvania, and Ohio, the Bay State has no shortage of god-awful municipalities. Even its crown jewel, Boston, is regarded by those in the know (i.e., people who've ever been to New York City) as the most provincial, cultureless, and puritanical excuse for a supposedly major city this side of Tehran. In fact, an exploration of the fifty worst places in Massachusetts could easily fill its own book (stay tuned).

How then, does lowly, insignificant Fitchburg manage to seize the crown? By competing on the national stage. Not content merely to wallow in its own immediate, local realm of crap, Fitchburg has worked hard to become a fixture on the American Worst Places to Live Circuit, regularly vying with such unbelievable shitholes as Glens Falls, New York, Birmingham, Alabama, and even the undisputed king, Yuba City, California, for worst-of-the-worst honors. By putting their collective noses to the grindstone, the people of Fitchburg have created a hell-hole for the ages, even by Massachusetts standards.

Quotes

For my money, the cruddiest place in the state is Fitchburg. Back in the seventies and eighties, the state took advantage of some federal program for settling refugees, and that is why so many of these old mill towns are now filled with Cambodians and Laotians. Yes, let's take chilly places of extreme poverty and no opportunity and bring in penniless people coming from tropical, war-ravaged countries. How benevolent. I guess Wellesley was full.

—Andrew G. Buckley

Fitchburg, the crappiest city ever! It's in North Central Massachusetts, and though I never lived there, I did work there for a year and seven months at the local newspaper (the *Sentinel and Enterprise*), which has its office right downtown. The place is just awful. It used to be a big industrial town, but then all the industry left, so it's just really depressed and bleak. It's actually really, really hilly (I remember one city official claimed it was the second hilliest urban area outside of San Francisco). That sounds like it would be nice, but instead there are just ramshackle houses that look like they're about to fall off these hills, and since it snows a ton during the winter (like everywhere else in New England), they cover the streets with salt and sand, since the roads have such steep inclines. So then, when it warms up, there are piles and piles of sand along the sides of the roads, and the city doesn't clean it up at all. It looks like they live in a desert, and all this sand swept into town. It's really weird. And there's tons of crime, of course.

—*Molly*

I passed through Fitchburg last July, when it was a balmy 98 degrees with no breeze. After maneuvering through all the auto parts scattered along the street, we drove into the center of town. Right there in the middle is this little, I don't know, park or square or common, and in the center of that there's a granite monument, like an obelisk, and I swear, it was as if Satan were sitting atop this pillar, casting fireballs and brimstone down on the town. Fitchburg is just irredeemable.

—*Stan R.*

F'boig was the home of the Captains of Industry back when central Mass actually had industry. It's now rotting away from the inside, like a grand old elm tree.

—*Scott Sanders*

Fitchburg is the last stop on one of the MBTA lines from Boston. Every now and then I'm sure a foreign traveler, accustomed perhaps to arriving at a major city and riding a train out to its last stop as a way of getting to know a new country, will pause with nauseous horror as he emerges from the train to see this city—its rotting bones stuck in the 1930s and its draping flesh a modern American tide pool for the socially abhorrent. It has become a joke of a city, populated mostly by toothless white people with greasy ragged hair and oily fingers. We called it "the Burg," and used the expression like it was a synonym for the joint or the slammer.

—*Andy Bayiates, www.andybandit.com*

PERFECTLY ILLUSTRATIVE HEADLINES FROM THE *SENTINEL AND ENTERPRISE*

- "Sex Offender Saw Porn Flick Near Day Care"
- "Cops Nab Suspect in Party Stabbings"
- "Alleged Drug Dealer Robs His Customers"

MICHAEL FENBERG

Gary, IN

Population: 102,746
Unemployment: 8.3%
Median Household Income: $27,195
Violent Crime Rate: 851.1
Climate: Smoggy
Ideal for: Gang Members, Out-of-Work Steel Workers, The Down and Out, The Forgotten
Cultural Highlights: Huffing Factory Exhaust, El-Train Graffiti, Murdering People at a Very High Rate, Rib Joints, Boxing, Basketball, Six-Packs (Beer, Not Abs), Abandoned Buildings

There is just one place
That can light my face.
　　—from the song "Gary, Indiana,"
　　in *The Music Man*

Named for Elbert Gary—lawyer, judge, and chairman of the board of U.S. Steel Corporation—the city of Gary, Indiana was actually founded by the company in 1906. The city's fortunes thus officially married to the steel giant, Elbert wasted no time establishing truly deplorable working conditions for the workforce, eventually culminating in the locally fabled labor strike of 1919, which served as Gary's greatest claim to fame until the Jackson Five were spawned some fifty years later.

Needless to say, that song is utterly preposterous, at least by the looks of present-day Gary, which has crumbled its way to becoming perhaps the single U.S. city least worthy of such glowing, musical appreciation.

Quotes

You want a shithole? Give Gary, Indiana, a try. When you drive anywhere east from Chicago, you have to pass through. You usually floor it, hold your breath to keep the toxic fumes from entering your lungs, and say a novena that you don't get shot. I remember once I was channel surfing and I came across the Black Miss America Contest, which was being held that year in Gary. I remember very clearly that the contestants were in a park in swimsuits with a forest of dead trees in the background.

—*Robert Powell*

It's where all the industry that Chicago rejected wound up. When you drive through on 80/90, all you see is steel mill after steel mill, chemical plant after chemical plant. You cannot avoid the smell of sulfur seeping into the car. The smokestacks, with their polluting plumage, fill the horizon as you drive by. Most of the buildings downtown look like prisons, their windows obscured by bars (and we're talking thirty-to-fifty-story buildings). The crime rate is disastrous, as is the median income. It's extremely dirty, too. If you must visit, bring galoshes or risk stepping in something nasty.

—*Sean MacCarthy*

I recall driving through it on the way to Chicago and having the impression that the entire town was covered with an inch of industrial soot.

—*Anonymous*

It's like an A bomb went off and the survivors still live there.

—*Michael Fenberg*

WIKIPEDIA SAYS . . .

"In the Chicagoland area, Gary is often reputed to have a distinctive odor due to its pollution, and it is the target of many jokes and comments. The large sign upon entering Gary from the west on Interstate 90—THE GARY SEWAGE TREATMENT DISTRICT WELCOMES YOU—does little to discourage these jokes. In 2004, Gary was awarded the title of 'America's Third Most Dangerous City' by the Morgan Quitno Corporation."

WISHFUL THINKING BY THE CHAMBER OF COMMERCE

- "The future of Gary is now! Don't miss it!"
- "Gary is preparing to be a technological superpower."

Look away, it's hideous!

Gatlinburg, TN

Gateway to the Smokies

Population: 3,382
Unemployment: 6.8%
Median Household Income: $37,606
Violent Crime Rate: 484.6
Climate: Suffocating
Ideal for: Tourists, Hefty Midwesterners, Christians, RV Owners, Masochists, Screaming Kids, Budget Travelers, The Blind
Cultural Highlights: Souvenirs, Gyp Joints, Freak Shows, Kitsch, Crap, Long Lines, Heat, Third-Rate Country Music, Trash

There are tourist traps and then there's Gatlinburg, Tennessee. What should be an idyllic hamlet perched on the edge of the Great Smoky Mountains National Park has instead, with help from its partner in crime, nearby Pigeon Forge (proud home of Dollywood), managed to produce a landscape of kitsch capitalism ostentatious enough to make Niagara Falls blush. A veritable magnet for fat people in short shorts and double-wide strollers fit to bursting with their obnoxious, popsicle-stained off-spring, Gatlinburg is an assault on both the senses and the wallet. By cramming the obscure and strange pleasures of a rambling road trip into the confines of several city blocks, this disaster of a town strips away the thrill of discovery until all that's left is a dull series of photo ops surrounded by traffic, heat, and the unbearable specter of endless tchotchkes. Do yourself a favor and keep driving.

Quotes

Gatlinburg will blow your mind.

—*David Gordon Green*

The ugliness intensified to fever pitch as I rolled into Gatlinburg, a community that had evidently dedicated itself to the endless quest of trying to redefine the lower limits of bad taste. . . . It made Cherokee look decorous. There is not much more to it than a single mile-long main street, but it was packed from end to end with the most dazzling profusion of tourist clutter.

—*from* Lost in America *by Bill Bryson*

This is the standard by which all Tourist Traps must be measured. Pigeon Forge and sister tourist-town Gatlinburg sparkle like junk jewels on a necklace choking Great Smoky Mountains National Park. Statistical density hampers attempts to successfully assess the situation, as a hundred attractions crush your sense of proportion and dignity. There's no way to see everything, and no way you would want to. Our best single penetration topped out at six or seven attractions before we beat a hasty retreat for oxygen. The Pigeon Forge experience naturally flows into the older resort town of Gatlinburg, nestled in a forested pass. Sit in the traffic jam on Gatlinburg's main street as massive gravitational forces push the mountains, factory outlet stores, and overweight pleasure zombies in on all sides of your car. Park if you can, and see the sights. Fudge being made. Laser tag. Four Ripley's-owned attractions. A Jesus-head sculpture whose eyes follow you. Low, low factory outlet prices.

—*roadsideamerica.com*

A SHORT CATALOGUE OF LOCAL ATTRACTIONS (IN ORDER OF MOUNTING HORROR)

1. World of Illusions—This glorified wax museum relies heavily on smoke and mirrors to achieve what little sense of thrill it manages to provide.

2. Ripley's Believe It or Not! Museum—Not so terrible until one realizes that the Ripley's company has established a virtual crap empire in Gatlinburg. After taking in the museum, be sure to avoid Ripley's Aquarium of the Smokies, Ripley's Davy Crockett Mini Golf, Ripley's Haunted Adventure, Ripley's Moving Theater, and Ripley's Super Funzone.

3. Hauntings—This one-of-a-kind theater extravaganza features objects and lights that "mysteriously" move around (the type of thing known to thrill audiences circa 1870).

4. Cooter's Place—Sure, everyone loves the *Dukes of Hazzard,* but most of us got over the urge to hang out at Cooter's garage sometime around our ninth birthday. Plus, no Daisy.

5. Victorian Gardens Wedding Chapel—In yet another attempt to co-opt the defining characteristics of other cities (check out the Seattle-esque Space Needle, if you must), Gatlinburg features many Vegas-style wedding chapels, of which the

Victorian claims to be the premiere edition. Don't forget: Christians only.

6. Hillbilly Golf—Learn about local culture while putting your way through a sensitively designed series of painstakingly recreated moonshine stills and outhouses. Hillbilly Golf: where fake ethnography meets pseudo entertainment!

7. Elvis Presley Museum—Elvis lives, or at least his trash does, at this memorabilia mecca, where fans can thrill to the King's razor, hair dryer, underwear, aftershave, and two sets of X-rays.

8. Salt and Pepper Shaker Museum—Have you ever wanted to take a look at seventeen thousand salt and pepper shakers? Didn't think so.

9. Christus Gardens—Spend the afternoon among busloads of Christian wackos as you enjoy this interactive demonstration of the Life of Christ. It's like being sucked into the television set during a late-night slate of evangelical programming. Of course, the gift shop and admission fee function in direct opposition to Christ's teachings.

The fun and excitement of downtown Glens Falls.

LINDSEY DUVALL

Glens Falls, NY

Gateway to the Adirondacks

Population: 14,354
Median Household Income: $30,222
Ideal for: Conservatives, The Elderly, Frustrated
Teens, White Trash (often drunk), Neohippies,
Hardcore/Metal Kids, Aging Baby Boomers,
Ultraconservatives, Crazy Nate (the Town Crazy),
Egotistical Aging Musicians, Pickup-Driving Hicks,
People Obsessed with Babies

Boredom takes many forms, chief among them Glens Falls, New York, a city so at peace with its own lack of amenities that it has no qualms mooching off the superior attributes of surrounding towns. Just as parts of New Jersey define their own self-worth according to their proximity to Manhattan, Glens Falls rationalizes its shortcomings by fixating on geography. Despite being crammed between two tourist areas, Glens Falls has absolutely nothing special to show for it, unless one counts its thoroughly mediocre civic center. Sure, Glens Falls sucks, but Saratoga Springs and Lake George are just around the corner!

Quotes

Glens Falls is home to the High School Basketball Hall of Fame, as well as to lost dreams and failed aspirations.

—*Patrick O'Grady*

Glens Falls is like a big, boring ghetto no one wants to stay in once the warm weather comes, because there's simply very little to do. So, in order to bring in tourists, Glens Falls will mention the surrounding area, *especially* Lake George. In fact, I'm sitting fifteen minutes north of Glens Falls, watching a Glens Falls cable network, and seeing a commercial for all the fun things to do in Lake George! Oh, the fun water, beach, shopping, boating, fireworks . . . it also feeds off of Lake George's Americade every June, hoping to bring in all those motorcyclists for shopping. The two local papers always mention the Washington County Fair, as well, which, if memory serves, is located in Greenwich, a half hour south. Generally, Glens Falls tries to pretend it's Saratoga, then in the summer it pretends it's an extension of Lake George.

To do anything, it's almost a half-hour drive. There is a park and a public library, but otherwise it consists of a hospital, a ghettoish housing development, some rich homes, a few small schools, churches, and a main strip that is nothing but bars and bums and a cheap, run-down motel known for drug use and fighting. The main thing to do here is shop—in an adjacent "town" called Queensbury, which possesses a slowly dying mall.

Also, it's kind of a hopeless area. Once you're here, you're stuck here, usually forever. People just lose hope; the jobs are terrible (mostly mill work, factory work, or retail and food service), wages are minimum, and it's near impossible to live comfortably. Everyone just gives up and has a bunch of kids out of boredom, so it winds up being pretty welfareish.

All the young people hate it here, and out-of-state visitors run away in fear, afraid of the supernatural powers of the town: its seemingly strong ability to cause depression, catatonia, psychosis, and many other fun, sometimes psychosomatic, illnesses.

—*Lindsey Duvall*

 MEANS OF ESCAPE

If you find yourself stuck in Glens Falls, don't panic. Remain calm and remember that the feelings of confusion, dread, depression, and angst you're currently experiencing are shared by everyone in town. Disillusionment and self-doubt are not only perfectly normal, but are in fact integral to the Glens Falls experience. Still, it's important to get out as quickly and judiciously as possible. The following methods should help expedite your mad dash back to civilization:

- GGFT Bus: For a mere seventy-five cents, this local bus line will whisk you away to the lovely confines of Lake George. For that price, sitting on a bus filled with Glens Falls natives doesn't even sound so bad.

- FAME Service: If you happen to be disabled, this door-to-door service will pick you up and make a special trip anywhere in the regular GGFT route. Some sort of certification is required (the bastards), but anyone with access to a wheelchair can probably talk their way onboard.

- Greyhound: It's hard to say what's worse: Greyhound or Glens Falls. Probably the latter.
- Amtrak: Hightail it to the "historic" Fort Edward train station, acquire an obscenely overpriced ticket, and the next thing you know, you'll be back in New York, Canada, wherever.
- Albany International Airport: The ultra-savvy traveler should endeavor to make his/her way forty-five minutes south, jump on a plane, and pretend this whole thing never happened.

A typically atrocious Granite City vista.

Granite City, IL

Population: 31,301

Median Household Income: $35,615

Ideal for: Steel Mill Employees, Wife Beaters, Potheads, Ultra-trashy Trailer Trash, Dirty Half-dressed Kids, Obnoxious Churchgoers, Pentecostals, High School Soccer Stars, Hoosiers, Derelicts

Cultural Highlights: Country Bar Karaoke, Train Racing, Bowling, Busch Beer, Binge Drinking, Bar-Sponsored Softball, NASCAR, Abortions, The Pumpkin Patch, Trans-Ams, April Snowstorms, Granite

With a name like Granite City, it's got to be good. Right? Not so fast. Though often overshadowed by neighboring East St. Louis in terms of sheer, mind-blowing despair, Granite City seems somehow worse, if only because expectations are slightly higher. While not an out-and-out ghetto, this blue-collar mill town is remarkable for the breadth and scope of its shortcomings, and for the way a palpable coat of failure seems spread across the city and its people.

Quotes

I was born and raised in Granite City, a small town just east of St. Louis on the other side of the Mississippi River. This is a very racist town full of white trash red-necks. Most of the people who live there earn their income working at one of the two huge steel mills that pollute the air so badly that the sky is always grey. I didn't know the sky was blue until I moved to Los Angeles. When I was a kid and would go to places with clean air, I'd get sick. Granite City is located in Madison County, which has the highest number of medical law-suits in the country.

There have been and may still be in place some very wacky laws, like for every bar in town there must be a church and African Americans were not allowed to own or rent property until 1994. I graduated from Granite City High School. In a class of about 350, there were 9 or 10 black kids. There were two Asians and I was scared of them at the time because I had never been exposed to other cultures.

There isn't much crime in Granite City, but that's only because the people are too unimaginative and lazy to try anything. The big hangout spots in Granite City are grocery store parking lots, IHOP, and Wal-Mart. There is a movie theater, but most people avoid it at all costs and drive a half hour to a decent theater.

Because of all the steel mills, you cannot get from point A to point B without crossing railroad tracks. The best part about this is that of course the crossing gates are always broken and stuck down, so you have to walk around them. A lot of people get killed that way. The problem is so bad that they show a safety video about it in high school driving class.

Since leaving, I have traveled around and seen a large portion of this country and other countries. I would have to say that of all the places I've ever been, Granite City is by far the worst. And, as if it's not horrible enough on its own, Granite City lies just to the north of East St. Louis, easily one of the worst cities in America.

—*Beth Dowell*

There is so much wrong with Granite City, it's hard to pinpoint all the things that make it suck so bad. It's just Granite City as a whole, like everything Granite City touches becomes tainted. Go to a Taco Bell in Granite City and I guarantee the food tastes worse than it does at any Taco Bell you've ever been to. But the people here don't care. It's like all the pollution spewing out of the steel mill has made them too perpetually ignorant to even notice.

Even the local hospital is horrible. I broke my knee and had X-rays taken, which I then took to Barne's Hospital in Saint Louis. There, the X-rays had to be completely redone, since the Granite City equipment was so primitive as to be useless. It's unreal. But hey, at least we're the Meth Capitol of the Midwest!

—*Jesse Dylan*

Here are a few helpful facts about Granite City:

1. Granite City was created solely for the purpose of making steel and is the fourth largest producer of steel in the United States.
2. Its three large steel factories are currently hard at work, but can and do close at a moment's notice. This has the effect of driving a quarter of Granite City's residents out of work.
3. Due to poor pollution controls, some people say the average high school graduate probably has the lungs of a pack-a-day, five-year smoker.
4. Though once a proud center of Klan activity, the region's general decline has brought with it a large influx of minorities, thus eroding the Klan's resources.
5. The BAC acronym for local junior Belleville Area College was usually referred to as "Bring a Crayon."

With accreditation it changed its name to Southwestern Illinois College and is now known as "Still Writing in Crayon."

6. The police chief announced a few years back that the city would no longer be arresting drunk drivers, as it caused too much paperwork.

7. Granite City has the second highest insurance rate in Illinois, second only to Chicago.

But to truly understand why Granite City sucks, you have to live in this area. The people are either elitist or stuck in a time warp. You've never seen so many mullets and old Trans-Ams. Its once beautiful downtown is now a ruined, postapocalyptic battleground. It was simply easier to let the old buildings fall apart than upgrade them. As a boy, I often went to see movies in the Washington Theater. It was one of the grand old movie places and would have easily received landmark status if anyone had cared . . . but of course no one did. All the really good restaurants left town years ago and the closest thing to a coffee shop is McDonald's.

—*Mark Purkaple*

SOCIAL ITINERARY

The next time you're in Granite City, do what the locals do. The following itinerary details a typical night in GC, with emphasis away from the town's more touristy attractions (whatever those might be). And remember, the strong evangelical Christian element will attempt to spoil your fun at every turn, so be sure to avoid them!

- 6:30 p.m.: Root around for spare change under couch cushions.
- 7:00 p.m.: Page dealer.
- 7:01 p.m.–7:25 p.m.: Wait for dealer to arrive.
- 7:25 p.m.: Score.
- 7:28 p.m.: Get stoned.
- 8:30 p.m.: Drive to Imo's (preferably one in St. Louis, not the pale Granite City imitation branch).
- 8:40 p.m.: Show off Trans-Am in parking lot. Ogle rival's Iroc-Z.
- 8:55 p.m.: Gorge on pizza.
- 9:30 p.m.: Hit the adjacent bowling alley for a few frames.
- 11:30 p.m.: Grab nachos from 7–11 on way home.
- 12:15 a.m.: Pass out.

VIRGE T. OWENS

Soon to be appearing on a hamburger bun near you.

Greeley, CO

Population: 76,930
Median Household Income: $36,414
Climate: Odiferous
Ideal for: Carnivores, Farm Folk, Slaughterhouse
Workers, Men with Mullets, Women With BIG Hair,
People Who Don't Mind Smelling Like Shit,
Washed-up Cowboys, Republicans
Cultural Highlights: E. coli, Death Metal Goat Roasts,
Broncos Games, Duck Hunting, Quarter Night at
the Local Saloon, Rodeos, Road Trips to Denver,
The Outlet Mall in Loveland

Greeley is where cows go to die and people go to kill them. It is a society based on slaughter, and the smell of death hangs heavily in the air. Long the butt of regional jokes ("a city of wide streets and narrow minds"), the town achieved a certain level of national infamy thanks to the book *Fast Food Nation,* which depicted conditions at the local ConAgra meatpacking plant in vivid and horrific detail.

Not content to merely stink to high heaven, Greeley is also a hotbed of gang violence and boasts a crumbling downtown whose most recognizable landmark was an abandoned Kmart.* Originally intended as a communist utopian community, the best that can be said about present-day Greeley is that some days don't smell quite as bad as others.

Quotes

When you think of Colorado, you think mountains, beautiful scenery, and skiing. While there are many towns in Colorado that don't feature any of these attractions, Greeley might be the worst of them. Fifty miles northeast of Denver, Greeley is situated on the plains and has more in common with Nebraska or Kansas than with Colorado. While the lack of scenery is tough, what's worse is that Greeley is home to one of the largest

*Good news for Greeley: In March 2006, 250 town residents showed up to celebrate the demolition of the old Kmart.

beef packing plants in the country. To support this plant, Greeley is also home to a very large feedlot. Unfortunately, the plant and the feedlot are located on opposite ends of town. Depending on which way the wind blows, you smell burnt blood or cow shit. When I attended the University of Northern Colorado in Greeley, the smell some nights was so bad you would literally have to put cologne under your nose so you could sleep. The smell was so bad, my parents refused to visit me at school. Instead, I had to meet them in Denver. The people of Greeley are friendly, stereotypical "Westerners" or plains people. Plenty of denim and big belt buckles . . . friendly people, but not very happy.

—*Alan Stanwick*

The one thing Greeley is known for is its smell of cows: live cows, dead cows, and cow poo. When I drive through Greeley, the smell gets in my air-conditioning vents and seeps out for about a day. Residents say they don't smell anything, but that's because they're in denial and have just gotten used to it.

—*Erin Barnes*

Greeley should be in the thesaurus for the word "shit": you get within twenty miles of the town and slam into a brick wall of stink from the feedlots and slaughterhouses of ConAgra and Montfort. Mmmmmmm . . . nothing like the stench of boiling cow blood and acres of cow shit to remind you of home. It *reeks* so badly that I choke whenever we drive in, while my husband (a native) sniffs the air and says "Ah, home," like he's smelling Toll House cookies or something. The first time I smelled the rendering plant, I thought something had crawled under my mother-in-law's house and died—I literally walked all around the house looking for a dead cat or rodent. Even the city parks are full of shit, albeit goose shit. You can't walk or sit on the grass because every migrating goose from Canada makes an annual Greeley pit stop. Must be the good ol' smell of shit that brings 'em in.

—*Samantha*

YES, IT REALLY SMELLS THAT BAD

Lest anyone doubt that Greeley actually stinks on a level otherwise unknown in modern times (Staten Island excluded), note that an Odor Hotline is up and fully operational. The City of Greeley's Planning and Zoning Division's Web site offers the following helpful information:

> To report an offensive outdoor odor, call the Odor Hotline at (970) 350-9831 between 7:00 a.m. and 11:00 p.m. as soon as it is noticed. Please leave your name, address, phone number, as well as the location where you detected the odor—if different from your address—an accurate description of the odor and its intensity, along with the direction the wind was blowing.

IT'S WHAT'S FOR DINNER

After the ConAgra Beef Company, Greeley's home-town corporate villain, was found to have produced the tainted meat responsible for Colorado's 2002 E. coli scare, company officials conscientiously responded by cooking most of the recalled meat, repackaging it, and reselling it in the form of canned chili, pet food, and similar products (unlabeled, of course).

 CONTRIBUTIONS TO AMERICANA

The famous phrase, "Go West, young man, go West" was penned by *The New York Tribune*'s Horace Greeley in support of the formation of a Utopian community that eventually became Greeley, Colorado.

Greenville, MS

Heart and Soul of the Delta

Population: 41,633
Unemployment: 7.7%
Median Household Income: $25,928
Violent Crime Rate: 991.7
Former Industry of Choice: Manual Labor
Ideal for: Street Corner Consultants, Tamale
    Connoisseurs, Debutante Crack Heads, Felonious
    State Representatives

Perched on the banks of the mighty Mississippi, Greenville is the largest and perhaps most noteworthy municipality in the Delta. Which is a bit like being the skinniest kid at fat camp, for the Delta, fabled birthplace of the blues, jazz, and rock 'n' roll, has seen better days, its flatlands and fertile soil ravaged by decades of eco-

---

GREENVILLE: ENTERTAINMENT
Most Popular Riverboat Casino Promotions

- Spin The Welfare Check Wheel
- Separate But Equally Loose Slots
- Christ Our Lord Keno
- Whistlin' Dixie Video Plantation Poker
- Crumbling Economy Cocktail Specials

---

nomic decline. Sometimes called the most Southern place on earth, the region does maintain a certain air of mystery. The Delta's got personality, all right. Unfortunately, it's also got one of America's worst standards of living, with jobs scarce, opportunity nonexistent, and most agriculture tied up in the hands of a few corporate behemoths. This is an area bordering on disaster, and an area of which Greenville claims to be the heart and soul.

Quotes

Mississippi's Delta region, unless one actually visits, is virtually impossible to describe in words. While it's perhaps unfair to single out one city or town as the worst, I'll do so anyway. Once you go west of Yazoo City (which is actually quite nice and attractive), you are in the Delta. Gone are the rolling hills and trees, replaced by cotton and catfish farms. Both require very flat land, and the Delta does not disappoint. Flat, brown, and unremarkable, the Delta is simply "the Delta"; no matter whichever specific point on the map you may be located, you are, first and foremost, in the Delta. The one town that is one of the crappiest in America would be Greenville. As you drive into town, you see nothing but seriously run-down shacks: shotgun shacks and small shanties with plastic sheets for windows and makeshift roofs. Then, out of nowhere, a beautiful five-bedroom home appears, situated on some beautifully maintained land. Immediately, the shacks return, the pattern repeating itself clear across town.

Greenville is situated on the Mississippi River, which in Mississippi terms means that casinos are permitted. Greenville has several riverboat casinos whose clientele are not, shall we say, what you might find in Vegas. These people make Atlantic City look like Beverly Hills. Sadly, most of the gamblers are cashing in their social security checks and spending whatever they can get their hands on, all in hopes of escaping the Delta.

Not surprisingly, when you mix poverty, unemployment, and no hope of leaving, you get crime. Yes indeed, Greenville, Mississippi, is not a place anyone would want to be after dark. The crime rate is staggering, comparable to that in Jackson, if not worse.

—*Alan Stanwick*

While Greenville does have an arts organization, and their chamber of commerce is real active ballyhooing that two-bit jazz festival they do, I guess it's so bad because it's so poor. Very, very few people there have any financial resources. Then they plopped down two gambling boats, the problem being that the "tourists" (i.e., people from Louisiana or Arkansas) go to Vicksburg, Natchez, or other places closer to the Arkansas state line, about fifty miles north. That leaves no one but locals to gamble in Greenville, as it's not geographically convenient for outsiders. So you've got your poor locals blowing their checks at the casinos. One Greenville casino let people come in every Friday to cash their check and get a free spin. Just imagine the consequences of *that*.

It's so racially tense in Greenville that no issue is free of it. My favorite detail was that the public library would keep the black-oriented magazines behind the counter, and you would have to go up and ask for them. Also, every single vote on the city council went along racial lines, even when there was no racial aspect involved. It's *that* kind of town, as are most southern towns now. And it is definitively southern. I never saw such scandal, nor eccentricity, as I did there. The people of Greenville are *very* proud of their two to three bars, their coffee shop, their gambling boats and, uh, their drug and alcohol addictions and messy affairs.

—*Delilah DeHaven*

Greenville is the unofficial capital of the Delta. It appears first as a series of signs rising above the cotton fields on Highway 82: Wal-Mart, John Deere, Taco Bell, Baskin-Robbins, Stogie Shoppe, Pawn Shop—Need Money Stop Here!

—*Jay McInerney, author*

WHAT'S ON GREENVILLE'S MIND: LETTERS TO THE EDITOR, *DELTA DEMOCRAT TIMES*

- **Bill of Rights Does Not Bar Display of Ten Commandments:** "This country was founded by Christian men based on Christian principles!"

- **Felt Was No Hero:** "W. Mark Felt [aka Deep Throat] was, and is, a traitor to both a president and to his chief . . . I say take the SOB to jail!"

- **Liberal Opinion Is Allowed, But It's Just Wrong:** "If you go back and look, when we took prayer out of public schools, our teen pregnancy rate, abortion rate, and crime rate went up. Do people not see the correlation? If we continue to remove God from our government, we will see our country slip into anarchy."

WISHFUL THINKING BY THE CHAMBER OF COMMERCE

- "The arts flourish in Greenville."

- "Making Greenville even more enticing is the wide range of cultural possibilities."

- "The perfect home is something everyone seeks. In the Greenville area, the search often takes no longer than a quick ride around town."

DENNIS RAY PAUL

Harrison, AR

Population: 12,152
Median Household Income: $27,850
Climate: Conservative
Ideal for: Caucasians, Grand Dragons, Militiamen, Hill
  People, Meth Addicts, Country Folk, Interlopers
Cultural Highlights: Antigovernment Activism, Hard-
  Line Christian Ideology, Cross Burning, Small-Town
  Charm

The seat of good ol' Boone County, Harrison, Arkansas, is a prime example of that sprawling backwater known as the Ozarks. Peopled mostly by descendents of Whiskey Rebellion distillers, this highland area enjoys a longstanding relationship with contraband, though moonshine has in recent years been replaced by methamphetamine. The pioneer spirit and rugged individualism that settled the frontier remain central to Harrison's wonderful sense of flair. Today, that same American sense of determination is evident in the area's insular worldview and radical extremist activity. Whether it's resentment of government interference, fanatical worship of Jesus, or that old chestnut, the persecution of blacks and Jews, Harrison has it all!

Quotes

Harrison is the headquarters for the KKK and extreme right-wing religious groups like Christian Identity. With the exception of Fayetteville and Eureka Springs, Arkansas, the Ozarks are an antebellum hellhole. The difference between Harrison and Springfield, Missouri, is that Harrison doesn't try to put on a happy face. Outsiders immediately know that they are not welcome or safe. Springfield sneaks up on you—but it's just as deadly."

—*Jeff Biener and Mary Meriam, ozarkopathy.org*

↗

A COMPLETELY DIFFERENT SPIN:

I grew up on a dairy farm just south of Harrison. When my friends and I were fifteen, we would walk a mile down to the store at Highway 65 to get a bottle of pop. We would stand along the highway and try to get the truck drivers to honk their horns. I had read all the books in the school library, but didn't even guess that there was a road that led out of Harrison. I didn't know that you could get to all those other places.

Harrison was always twenty years behind the rest of the world. To listen to modern rock and roll, you had to stay up late and wait till the local station went off the air. Then you could get WLS from Chicago on the AM part of the radio. Now that it is starting to catch up, well, to me it's lost its innocence. They say that for the rest of the country, the fifties was when they lost their innocence. I always thought the seventies was when Harrison lost its.

I remember going to town with no shirt, just britches and tennis shoes, and not feeling out of place. And of course a straw hat. No one was dressed without their hat. We would go to the feed store and the owner would give me a dime to get a pop. Most of those people have died now. Some of the people replacing them are people that I grew up with, but others are recent arrivals from out of state.

They came to have a better way of life, to live slower and have cheaper taxes. Then they start changing things here to the way they were in the place they left. They miss all the utilities and having people do things for them. All the things that were quaint when they visited are now bothersome quirks of an antiquated society. So they pass laws and keep changing things till they have the same problems that they had where they came from.

I was born and raised here and wouldn't want to go somewhere else and try to get to know the rules there. People jump in here and start changing things without knowing the rules. The original people were friendly, but suspicious of outsiders. Now it is unusual to meet people from Harrison. It may not be hardly that bad, but there are many newcomers. I am glad to see the new business and industry coming in, but I am sad at the same time. I miss the old ways and the old times, when you could walk along the highway trying to get the truckers to honk their horns. The drive-in theater and chasing girls all night, not knowing what you would do with one if you caught up to them. All that is gone now, or at least the drive-in is. Maybe I just miss my youth, and the friends from those times. They were great.

—Dennis Ray Paul

CHRISTIAN IDENTITY, THE KLAN, AND YOU

One of the more noteworthy things about Harrison, Arkansas, is that it functions as the headquarters of the Knights of the Ku Klux Klan, which just happens to be the largest faction of the KKK. Though the Klan's popularity continues to wane (even in Arkansas), modern Harrisonians have embraced Christian Identity, an ultra-right-wing extremism for the new millennium. Perfectly tailored for the racist who loves Jesus, Christian Identity is something of an ideological partner of the Klan's, similarly obsessed but without the pomp and circumstance. Keep this in mind the next time you drop in for Sunday services.

 WISHFUL THINKING BY THE CHAMBER OF COMMERCE

- "Many area residents and visitors enjoy the relaxation and excitement of motorcycling in the Ozarks."
- "The perfect climate for business and pleasure."

PERFECTLY ILLUSTRATIVE HEADLINES FROM THE *HARRISON DAILY TIMES*

- "Recovery from Meth Hard, But Possible"
- "Belief in God Not 'Whacked Out'"

Helena, MT

Heart of the Rockies

Population: 25,780
Median Household Income: $34,416
Formerly Known As: Crabtown
Ideal for: Single Moms, Farm Folk, People Operating Under the Mistaken Impression That This Is a Big City
Cultural Highlights: Chain Restaurants, Drinking, Long Weekends, Short Work Days, Summer Block Parties, Ghost Towns

State capitals are usually a pretty safe bet. Even in the most dreadful states, the capital city can be counted on to provide something of a metropolitan and worldly experience, at least relatively speaking. Then there's Montana, whose feeble attempt at a capital can't even live up to the rest of the state. And we're talking about Montana, which isn't exactly *the* place to be to begin with. But at least it's pretty, which is sort of something. Helena, on the other hand, is little more than a way station, a pit stop of fleeting entertainment value. It's small, of scant historical interest, and boasts hiking as its most major attraction. Which is really just walking, if you think about it.

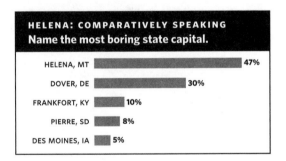

HELENA: COMPARATIVELY SPEAKING
Name the most boring state capital.

HELENA, MT	47%
DOVER, DE	30%
FRANKFORT, KY	10%
PIERRE, SD	8%
DES MOINES, IA	5%

Quotes

Helena, Montana, must be the worst place on the planet to live. For starters, there are only about twenty thousand people who live in the area, yet they think it's New York City. Most of the people have never been out of Montana and consider the Dakotas to be on the East Coast. If you want to go out for dinner on a Sunday, forget it. Everything is closed, with the possible exception of Applebee's. Generally, local businesses are only open from about 10:00 a.m. until 3:30 p.m. On Fridays, everyone shuts up shop at 3:00 and disappears for the weekend. My junior high curfew was less restricting.

I first arrived in Montana on a Thursday night, which is typically a big night in a college town (Carroll College is located in Helena). Exhausted from my drive, I met up with a coworker and we went to a bar called the Rialto, a run-down dive bar with about five people in it. This place was straight out of the fifties; there were red leather chairs, dust and grime everywhere. Not what I'd call a great college bar. While there, someone remarked that it was kinda crowded. On Saturday nights, the big place to go is called Bullwhackers, located in the lobby of the Holiday Inn. For a five-dollar cover charge, you can drink huckleberry beer and listen to a variety of music, from new rap (which is actually three years old) to all the hillbilly country you can handle.

The weather in Helena is atrocious. It snows until the end of May, then on June first the temperature shoots up to over 100. It stays light until almost 10:00, and since nobody seems to know what air-conditioning is, it's downright miserable. In September, the temperature drops right back down to 30 and it resumes snowing. During the summer, the entire valley is covered by plumes of smoke from the numerous forest fires raging nearby. I worked for the minor league baseball team and we once had a lady call the league office to complain that we were playing despite the poor air quality. We called the local TV station and spoke with their forecaster (they didn't have an actual meteorologist), who told us that the air quality wasn't even into the moderate zone, despite the smell.

The country song "Small Town Saturday Night" by Hal Ketchum is all about Helena. The one movie theater only has a single screen and shows old movies over and over again. The locals buy billboards as anniversary presents and as memorials when people die. Helena shuts down every year for the Last Chance stampede and fair, which is basically a rodeo everyone thinks is the greatest thing to ever happen and a crowd of three thousand is considered the largest gathering of all time.

—*Mike Snow*

PERFECTLY ILLUSTRATIVE HEADLINES FROM THE *QUEEN CITY NEWS*

- "Hobo Spiders Hitching Rides in Helena"
- "College 'Uninvites' Planned Parenthood Representative"
- "METH = DEATH"

Houston, TX

Space City
Bayou City
H-Town

Population: 1,953,631
Median Household Income: $36,616
Violent Crime Rate: 768.8
Climate: Like the fiery pits of hell
Ideal for: Satan, Deadly Competitive Cheerleader
Moms, Violent Housewives, Shady Corporate
Executives, The Overweight, Over-the-Hill
Cowboys, Illegal Aliens, Christians

Cultural Highlights: Air-conditioning, Sunday Services (with stadium seating and pyrotechnics), The Rodeo, 4H Club, BBQ Joints, Second-Rate Mardi Gras, Beauty Pageants, Public Transportation Fatalities, Football, Strip Clubs

Houston is the fourth largest city in the United States, behind only New York, Los Angeles, and Chicago. Consider also Philadelphia (at number five) and one thing becomes abundantly clear: Houston is by far the worst major city in America. Ugly, sprawling, and, come summer, outrageously hot and humid, Houston feels more like a gigantic corporate park than a vibrant metropolis. Seemingly plopped down at random, with little consideration paid such trivialities as urban planning or traffic management, the city sprawls on and on for what feels like forever, ultimately encompassing a treeless, flat expanse twice the size of Rhode Island. In case this doesn't sound bad enough, Houston also features the second-worst air quality in the United States.

Quotes

Houston boasts what might be the worst zoning in the entire country—houses sit on major interstates, factories reside next to neighborhoods, and the sprawl seems absolutely endless.

—*Sheldon Yeager*

I travel to Houston semi-often for business. After the first couple of trips, I realized there's absolutely no reason to leave the hotel. At least there's cable TV in my room. Outside, it's either raining or sweltering. Or some Houstonite directs us somewhere that's supposedly the nicest restaurant in town, which turns out to be average by New York standards. And just try getting drinks after dinner . . . *nothing* is open! I mean at 11:00 p.m.! Now I just eat breakfast, lunch, and dinner at the Four Seasons and wait impatiently until it's finally time for my return flight.

—*Stefanie*

The fine people of Houston have utterly failed to grasp the concept of merging. No one merges. Instead, they come to a complete stop, then sit there, confusedly looking about, eyes blinking in the bright sun like moles crawling up out of the earth. Finally, after growing suitably comfortable with the way a highway works, they consent to move forward, slowly, painfully. All the while, you're stuck behind them, honking and losing your mind.

Houston social life, if you can call it that, tends to revolve around two choices: the mall or barbecue. Mall . . . or barbecue. The local barbecue specialty is super tough, overcooked meat, accompanied by beer. Barbecue is just an excuse to drink beer, really. So the choice actually boils down to: mall or beer. It must be all the Methodists keeping the malls in business.

—*Katie*

Houston is so boring, there isn't even much to make fun of.

—*Lauren Key*

STATE RIVALRY TALE-OF-THE-TAPE

Houston shares something of a semifriendly rivalry with Dallas, its vastly superior neighbor to the north (vastly superior as far as Texas goes, anyway). Though it enjoys an edge in the rather mundane "population" category, H-Town is severely lacking on most other fronts. The following handy chart details Houston's shortcomings in wildly condensed form:

	Dallas	Houston
Sex Symbol	Cowboys Cheerleaders	Anna Nicole Smith
Fictional Icon:	J. R. Ewing	Troy Dyer
Landmark:	Texas School Book Depository	Astrodome
	Dallas	**Houston**
Physical Trait:	Sprawl	Sprawl
Annoying Celebrity:	Ashlee Simpson	Renee Zellweger
Football:	Cowboys	Texans

Physique:	Passable	Fattest City, 2005*
Criminals:	Bonnie and Clyde	Andrea Yates
Evil Corporation:	Exxon Mobil	Enron
Wild Card:	Jerry Jones's Plastic Surgery	No Zoning Laws

As the above chart plainly shows, Dallas is the clear winner in all categories save Annoying Celebrity, which is a toss-up.

Men's Fitness magazine

Jacksonville: where sun, fun, and homelessness collide.

Jacksonville, FL

Where Florida Begins

Population: 735,617
Median Household Income: $40,316
Violent Crime Rate: 1034.2
Climate: Only the rare hurricane
Times Featured on *COPS*: At Least Six
Ideal for: Relocated Ex-cons, Relocated Homeless People, Hopeless Drug Abusers/Alcoholics, Crack Whores

Cultural Highlights: Marital Infidelity, Unwanted Pregnancies, Chinese Buffets, Hard Narcotics, Liquor, Murder, Racism

Jacksonville is named for Andrew Jackson, seventh president of the United States and a man who supposedly never set foot in the area. Had he, chances are he probably would have requested they keep his name out of it. Jacksonville is the largest city in the United States in terms of land area, a purely mundane statistic that functions locally as an intense point of pride (it's virtually impossible to read anything about Jacksonville without crashing headlong into this factoid). Of course, by this logic Manhattan sucks, so take it as you may.

Fresh off serving as what many felt was the worst host city in Super Bowl history (with apologies to Houston, Texas), Jacksonville has at least made recent strides to step out onto the national stage. Of course, since most attending national journalists spent more time lamenting the city's lack of hotel rooms, taxis, decent restaurants, and anything even remotely resembling a downtown than they did covering the game, it might have been a better idea to continue flying under the radar.

Quotes

Jacksonville is like a Limp Bizkit video gone very, very wrong. There's something in the air that makes it feel as if there's a satanic slaughter happening just around every corner. Either that, or some sort of violent gangster festivities.

—Mike Tully

Jacksonville might be the worst-smelling city in the Western hemisphere.

—Alan Aiello

Jacksonville makes Tampa look like Paris.

—Tony Kornheiser, The Washington Post

PERFECTLY ILLUSTRATIVE HEADLINES FROM THE *FLORIDA TIMES-UNION*

- "Stripper's Body Still Missing"
- "Duval [County's] Math Scores Amid State's Worst"
- "Man Shot While Sitting on His Porch"
- "Officials: Sex Offender Ran Jacksonville Gynecological Clinic"

EAU DE JACKSONVILLE

Jacksonville's trademark stench is a masculine bouquet highlighted by earthy overtones. The fragrance opens with the stimulating, evanescent aroma of burnt coffee, creating an unmistakably powerful effect upon the senses. Its harmonized blend of woody, exotic swamp spices are lent greater depth by subtle notes of paper mill extract, resulting in an odor that's as intensely unsexy as the city itself.

Lake Placid's fully accredited Clown College, offering advanced degrees in juggling, face painting, and terrifying young children.

Lake Placid, FL

Caladium Capital of the World
Town of Murals

Population: 1,668
Median Household Income: $21,178
Ideal for: Clowns in Training, Vacationers on a Budget, Clog Dancers, Senior Citizens, Florists, Unbelievably Bored Teenagers, Migrant Workers
Cultural Highlights: Bird Watching, Flower Watching, Civic Pride Murals, Garbage Cans, Lakes, Empty Streets, Dusty Antiques, Annual Flower Festivals, Old Cars, Hard Labor, Citrus

You know things aren't going so well when a town's highlights include some sort of native plant and a series of murals intended to shed light on local history (and which boast such inspired titles as "Turpentine Industry," "Train Depot," and "Turkey Hunt—The Lost Opportunity"). Jeez, at least throw in a Hooters or something, like the rest of Florida does. And yet Lake Placid, a supposedly idyllic hamlet located in the center of the state, still manages to lure droves of visitors with the promise of quality entertainment on par with a seventh-grade arts and crafts show. How this can be possible is anyone's guess, though one may reasonably assume that the typical Lake Placid tourist lives somewhere even more boring.

Quotes

Lake Placid, Florida, is by far the crappiest town ever! Once you have driven through the first traffic light . . . that's it! You might as well keep on moving, because there is nothing else to see, except for the twenty-seven gator-infested, muddy lakes, of course. Uptown is downtown and downtown is uptown! Forget about a business district. Lake Placid is the "Caladium Capital" of the world? Oh wow! Excited yet? A caladium, by the way, is a heart-shaped plant, and you can only see so many before you're completely sick of them. They're everywhere! Yet something draws people to this little summer town of Lake Placid. In fact, some just can't get enough, and are drawn back again and again. It's a regular tourist trap!

The town has no mall, not even a Wal-Mart. I mean, doesn't every town have a Wal-Mart? Lake Placid has zilch as far as career opportunities are concerned, unless you want to be a cashier at the local grocery store or pick citrus under the sweltering Florida sun. Oh yeah, there's a lot of citrus, groves and groves and groves of it, which the police use to hide in and set speed traps. It took years before they even allowed a Burger King to be built in Lake Placid. Everything must be approved in a town meeting. Each year, the town holds its Caladium Festival, joy of all joys. The highlight of the festival, besides the caladiums, are the cloggers, who descend on Lake Placid to torture everyone with their country tap-dance routines. All the little old ladies love to clog.

The only thing for teenagers to do is drive out to what they like to call "The Sands," a pile of dirt where you can go "muddin'" with your dirtbike or pickup truck and a cold twelve-pack. Or there's one club, called Geckos, twenty minutes away. That's it. Wow!

Lake Placid is full of nosy neighbors, tobacco chewers, rude librarians, creepy murals, bad motels (there are only two), and overpriced homes. The town also has something called "The Happiness Tower," a kind of lookout spot where someone once committed suicide off of. Please, for your sake don't go to Lake Placid. It's anything but placid and it's in the the middle of nowhere!

—*D. Fettner*

If you're after some serious Florida outback, travel down U.S. Hwy 27, which runs from the Georgia border near Tallahassee all the way to Miami. There you will find towns (if you wish to call them that) that look like locations from the film *Easy Rider,* filled with inhabitants that fit the stereotypical Southern Good Ol' Boys' mold. One time I traveled this route and unfortunately had to stop for gas in a town called Lake Placid. I had to go inside to charge the gas, and when the woman saw my name on the credit card she said, "How do y'all say that name?" After about five minutes of trying to get her to pronounce it correctly, her next question was, "What country are y'all from? Oh, it's I-talian." I think she was afraid I was an Arab or Mexican. Needless to say, I got the hell out of there pretty fast. It was like they forgot the Civil War has been over for a hundred and fifty years already.

—*Alan Aiello*

WISHFUL THINKING BY THE CHAMBER OF COMMERCE

- "Any season of the year is a good time to visit Lake Placid."

- "Our Mural Society has also commissioned many whimsical trash containers. . . . Set aside time during your trip to take the walking tour of this unique feature of our community."
- "Lake Placid proudly claims to have more clowns per capita than any other town in Florida."

NATE HARGER

Depressed yet?

Lorain, OH

Population: 68,652
Median Household Income: $33,917
Climate: Even worse than Cleveland
Former Industries of Choice: Shipping, Steel
Ideal for: Hard-luck Former Professionals, Drunks on Bicycles, Women with Super-long Blond Hair and Forty-five Kids
Cultural Highlights: Stray Bullets, Abandoned Buildings, Unemployment Insurance, Sadness, Nudie Bars, Shuttered Nudie Bars, Junk Stores, Shuttered Junk Stores, Appliance Stores, Shuttered Appliance Stores, Church, The VFW

Past the western edge of Cleveland lies the port city of Lorain, or at least what remains of the port city of Lorain. To say Lorain is on the decline is like saying MC Hammer's street cred is waning. This is an armpit of the postindustrial model: industry leaves, money goes with it, and what's left behind is a still-populated shell of civilization. People carry on, sort of, though the after-glow of past glory taints everything. It's like an entire town full of ex–high school jocks who've gone on to pump gas and live in the past. Plus, it's got a whole bunch of crime for good measure.

Quote

It's like *Deliverance,* but urban.

—*Shelly R.*

Lorain was a one-industry, one-employer town. Then the employer either left or cut way back. It's a very depressing place now. My understanding is that the town once flourished as a Great Lakes shipping port (the original site of George Steinbrenner's American Shipbuilding Company) and became the site of a large steel mill that attracted laborers from all over the world. Then, the shipping business went away and the steel mill all but closed. Virtually nothing replaced them. So, today, my impression is that Lorain is a sad, poor little place with not much new going on. For a while, some politicians and developers wanted to build a casino there, but it was put to a statewide referendum and failed.

—*Anonymous*

LORAIN'S CONTRIBUTIONS TO AMERICANA

What would America be like without Lorain? Well, it would probably be pretty much the same. But then again . . . just try to imagine the state of things had Lorain not stepped up and churned out the following pillars of our society. Without Lorain, we might as well be living in Canada.

- **George Steinbrenner:** This famed shipping magnate and owner of the New York Yankees continues to exemplify the great American virtues of victory, greed, and hubris.
- **The Ford Econoline Van:** Born of Lorain's assembly lines, the Econoline is the vehicle of choice for discerning pedophiles everywhere. The next time you hear about a creepy, mustachioed man cruising the neighborhood with a van full of candy, thank Lorain!
- **Toni Morrison:** The Nobel prize–winning author's impressive body of work doubles as the bane of freshman lit majors everywhere.

- **Father Guido Sarducci:** Even funnier than real church, Father Guido Sarducci was a highlight of the old *Saturday Night Live* and still pops up from time to time, albeit in somewhat less humorous form.

Culture thrives in Manchester.

Manchester, NH

Queen City
Where History Invites Opportunity

Population: 107,006
Median Household Income: $40,774
Ideal for: Refugees, Drunks, Women with Eighties
   Bangs, Bikers and the Women Who Love Them,
   Skinhead Toughs, French Canadians, The
   Directionless, Aging Strippers

Cultural Highlights: Mullets and Moustaches, Bad Teeth, Cars with Bad Detail Work, Unce Unce Music, Dive Bars, The Red Arrow Diner, Milwaukee's Best, Natural Light, Sitting Around Watching Porn, Video Games

In 1998, *Money* magazine named Manchester, New Hampshire, the Number One Small City in the East. Huh? Kind of makes you wonder what the competition was. Bridgeport, Connecticut? Pawtucket, Rhode Island? Newark, New Jersey? At any rate, they must have been grading on a curve, because while Manchester might be masquerading as a reasonable place to live, the proof, as they say, is in the pudding. Or, in this case, in the outrageously harsh winters, or in the laughable arts scene, or in the fact that it's not even the best city in New Hampshire.

Quotes

Manchester manages to combine the essence of back-woods trailer trash, the bad weather of the Northeast, and all the sad things about real city life: homelessness, drugs, and disease.

—*George Millet*

Manchester sucks, but it sucks in a way that most small, remote-state cities suck. You sometimes can't blame it for its suckiness, since it really has no high bar to reach. Nobody expects a city in the middle of New Hampshire to be any good anyway. So it's sort of innately sucky. Perhaps what's most sad about Manchester is that it mimics Boston's most meatheaded establishments (like Jillian's, a giant arcade/bar/party place), but fills them with only New Hampshire meatheads, a lower breed than their Boston counterparts. Its major hotel/convention center was probably built in 1982 or earlier and they have this new stadium thing that's supposed to draw great bands and stuff, but in essence it's a sucky city. It's in between Boston and Portland. Boston is old and small, but an official city. Portland is tiny, remote, and charming. Manchester has big-city garbage and no charm.

—*Scott Moe*

Manchester is a very cheap place to live and is close enough to Boston that I didn't think it would be so bad, especially since I knew I'd only be there for one year. Boy, was I in for a surprise. Our bedroom was formerly the site of either a suicide or a murder (details remain sketchy), a fact the realtor had neglected to inform us of, but which made me feel right at home once I found out. The upstairs neighbors were absolutely rotten, electing to dispose of their empty Bud, Natural Light, and Milwaukee's Best cans in the stairwell. This created quite a wonderful stench in the summer. When not tossing beer cans down the stairs, they spent the majority of their time screaming at each other or neglecting their unwashed, underfed offspring.

Outside, things weren't much better. The streets were littered with bums strung out on crystal meth, obnoxious French Canadians, crusty old bikers, and these packs of highly annoying boys with pimped out VWs who cruised the neighborhood blasting bad techno and hip hop. For fun, people drank beer constantly. And they only drank the cheapest, most watered-down crap on the market, and always in cans. They consumed case after case. It was actually sort of impressive.

Other than that, there were endless dive bars, some of which even had illegal strippers that performed on Saturday and Sunday mornings! This was not only so they wouldn't lose weekend night business, but so the cops wouldn't be suspicious. I tried my best to make it work in Manchester, but it was a disaster. This city is practically unlivable.

—Annick

POP CULTURE CLAIMS TO FAME
- Manchester is the birthplace of Grace Metalious, the author of *Peyton Place*.
- The city serves as the hometown of President Jed Bartlett on NBC's *The West Wing*.
- Adam Sandler was raised in Manchester.

JAY TORBORG

Blinded by the crap.

Mitchell, SD

Population: 14,558
Median Household Income: $31,308
Climate: Tacky
High School Team Name: The Kernels
Ideal for: Corn Enthusiasts, Farmers, Shriners, Good Neighbors, Doll Collectors
Cultural Highlights: Corn, Creepy Dolls, Maze, Sowing, Harvesting, Rejoicing, Roadside Oddities/Giant Statues

Mitchell, South Dakota, is a prairie town obsessed with corn. Yes, that corn, the vegetable, the one on the cob. Obsessed to the point that its official Web site mentions (and provides a link to) the World's Only Corn Palace right there in the very first sentence, ahead of such trivialities as public works and safety information. In case you're still clamoring for more, there's another link to the Corn Palace's schedule on the bottom of the page. Plus, just to be safe, a third link is thoughtfully provided and prominently displayed in the menu left of screen. As for the strangely Russian-looking Corn Palace itself, well, the dirty secret is that it's not actually built from corn, just covered with it. Each year, during Corn Palace week, the place is decorated with a new series of pride-tastic murals, made from corn, grain, and other foodstuffs. Inside, the palace functions primarily as an auditorium and sports venue.

As if that weren't enough, directly across the street from the World's Only Corn Palace stands the Enchanted World Doll Museum, which "offers excitement, enchantment and education as you pass through the doors of this English-style castle, complete with moat, turrets and drawbridge," according to the Corn Palace Convention and Visitor's Bureau's Web site. If the thought of an entire building filled with dolls doesn't creep you out, then by all means give Mitchell a shot during your next road trip.

Quotes

Probably the most egregious example of kitsch capitalism run amok this side of Las Vegas, Mitchell has built its
economy around corn and features the internationally
unknown "Corn Palace," covered entirely with what
else? On a cross-country trip, I stopped to take a photo
of the roadside structure, at which point a carload of locals slowed down so that the driver could yell, "It's just
corn, you asshole!" before speeding off. Yeah, no shit. It's
an entire building of it.

—*Bill Griffith*

Mitchell's Corn Palace should be the poster child for
American consumerism. While people around the world
continue to starve to death, the fine folks of Mitchell,
South Dakota, are busy building tourist traps out of
food.

—*Mike Moocherelli*

THAT'S ENTERTAINMENT!

Now playing at the Corn Palace:

"The famous comedy duo is back! Williams and
Ree may bill themselves as 'The Indian and the
White Guy,' but their hilarious pointed jabs tend to
wander from their traditional Indian-White Guy
jokes to poking fun at everyone. Williams and Ree

will perform at the Corn Palace on Friday, April 29 at 7:00 p.m."

PERFECTLY ILLUSTRATIVE HEADLINES FROM THE *MITCHELL DAILY REPUBLIC*

- "2006 Palace Murals to Feature Rodeo Theme"
- "Walgreens Plans to Open Store in Mitchell"
- "Local Man Selling Off Collection of Tractors"

The result of Nampa's "Pave Everything" initiative.

Nampa, ID

Population: 51,867

Median Household Income: $34,758

Ideal for: Rednecks, Tough Guys, Exploitative Employers, Christians

Cultural Highlights: Teen Pregnancy, Flies, Mosquitoes, Workplace Injuries, Shootin' Stuff, Rodeo, Golf

Nampa is one of those places that, despite recent efforts to clean up its act, still falls horribly short. Not even a shiny, new city Web site (which Nampa has) is enough to turn things around. Despite adopting the slogan "What a Place to Live!" Nampa remains anything but, especially if you happen to be of bovine persuasion, in which case you'll promptly be slaughtered on the edge of town. Which is no knock on carnivores. After all, who in their right mind doesn't enjoy a tasty burger? Thing is, most of us don't need to live right next door to the rendering plant. Better we allow our meat products to retain some air of mystery, no? Well, no such luck in Nampa, where the Armour Fresh Meat Company plant fills the summer breeze with the stench of animal carcasses, and from which bloody animal parts (bones, guts, hides) exit the building via a conveyor belt located in plain view of the adjacent roadway.

It's hard to say who's got it worse, the cows, or the huddled masses of high school dropouts Nampa cranks out annually, whose prospects start with the meat plant and end with the sugar factory across town.

Quotes

I grew up in a shithole called Nampa, Idaho. The main industry was the White Satin sugar factory (or "White Satan," as we called it) that made the whole town smell like burning cat shit all winter long. There were also a bunch of smaller factories that paid minimum wage or not much better. At my elementary school, we had sing-along assemblies on Fridays. All the students would gather in a big auditorium to sing a song called, and I shit you not, "We are factory workers." It didn't occur to me until much later just how fucked up that song was. Nampa had a large Mexican migrant population, and fighting was a daily part of life. You fought your way to school, then fought your way home. So many fights ended with someone going to the hospital that it didn't seem abnormal until I got older and moved away. I was afraid of moving to a big city because of all the horror stories I'd heard, of gang wars and so on. So it came as some shock to discover how tame the urban ghettos are compared to my hometown.

—*Rob*

Although Nampa has tried to improve its image over the past couple of years, it's still a hole. My friend took me to Nampa's first "strip club," where the girls strip down to full-coverage bathing suits. Even thongs are illegal in Idaho. The "good" side of Nampa has seen a lot of growth . . . basically limited to some California-style strip-mall development, but there was a drive-by shooting on that side of town just a few weeks before I visited. They're twenty years behind the times on everything. Common fashions are still mullets and mall-bangs and camel-toes. Nampa High allowed students to smoke in shop class! It's still an extremely racist, backward place full of crime and religious dogma.

—*Jennifer W.*

I'll admit that Nampa looks nicer than it used to. They replaced a lot of the old city buildings with new ones: a new library, a new police station, a new city hall, a new event center, a new high school. The growth has come from some computer-part manufacturing that's moved in to the area. But the seedy underbelly is alive and well, and the old stink still lingers: cow carcass in the summer, burnt crap from the sugar factory in the winter. Also, it's important to keep in mind that Nampa is merely the centerpiece of a whole area full of smaller towns that are just as bad, if not worse. Caldwell is a twilight-zone sort of town; really, really scary at night. And Middleton is a redneck free-for-all.

—*Joe Michaels*

Nampa is full of macho idiots who hate fags and Mexicans and think the King James Bible supersedes the U.S. Constitution. An unwritten local rule dictates that a man with anything more than one earring in his left ear is automatically gay. Guys with both ears pierced can expect to suffer ass-kickings on a regular basis. When not beating on people, these rednecks enjoy driving out to the country and shooting anything and everything that moves, plus most stuff that doesn't. Take a drive outside of Nampa and you'll see the remains of rotting, dead rabbits everywhere. But watch out for beer-swilling, trucker-cap-wearing idiots shooting rifles from the back of a moving pickup truck. Interspersed around the carcasses are heaps of charming desert junk, like rusted, abandoned cars, dumped refrigerators, and old oil drums, all so full of bullet holes they look like Swiss cheese. Even the deer-crossing signs are riddled with bullet holes. I've even seen guys shooting at protected pelicans at Lake Lowell, a man-made reservoir where the rednecks like to shoot giant carp with guns and bows. In the winter, it freezes over and people drive out onto it and slide around. When I was a kid, some rednecks took their 4×4 out there and it fell through the ice and sunk to the bottom of the lake.

—*Jason*

WISHFUL THINKING BY THE CHAMBER OF COMMERCE

- "The heart of Idaho's wine country."
- "Nampa is always on the move . . ."

A DISSENTING OPINION (WITH HELPFUL SUGGESTIONS)

Nampa is not even close to being the worst town in Idaho. At least not when one considers these two:

- Pocatello—was once the second largest city in the state and home to a gigantic rail yard and a pair of phosphate mining companies. While there is a university in town—Idaho State University—the city now faces life without its largest employers. And it shows. It is probably one of the most depressing places I have ever been.

- Blackfoot—This Southeast Idaho town is just north of Pocatello and even more run-down. A thriving burg the week of Labor Day, when one of the state's largest fairs is in full swing, the rest of the year Blackfoot is known as Crapfoot. But they do offer 'Free Taters to Out of Staters' at the World Potato Expo, where you can take a photo on the giant concrete Idaho spud.

If you are talking basic livability, Nampa beats most of southeast Idaho.

—Seth Nickerson

North Platte, NE

Population: 23,878
Median Household Income: $34,181
Climate: Pretty barren and more than a little chilly
Ideal for: Prospective Californians, Those Satisfied
with the Status Quo, Pig Humpers, Mediocre Office
Drones, Christians
Cultural Highlights: Spoiled Yogurt, Coffee Shops
with Hand-Drawn Pictures of Christ on the Fridge,
Out-of-step Line Dancing, Buffalo Bill Cody's
Ranch, The Mall, Freezing

Make no mistake: North Platte, Nebraska, is God's country. As such, it's also boredom country. Perhaps the most interesting thing about North Platte is that it serves as a major freight train stopover. And that about covers it, unless one considers the fact that Buffalo Bill Cody spent several years in the area to be of interest. If so, North Platte's Fort Cody Trading Post (and Old West Museum) and Buffalo Bill's Miniature Wild West Show may provide some semblance of diversion, though visitors should be forewarned that the latter is comprised mainly of puny dioramas. Yes, they're hand carved, but still.

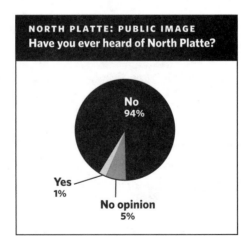

NORTH PLATTE: PUBLIC IMAGE
Have you ever heard of North Platte?

No
94%

Yes
1%

No opinion
5%

Quotes

I once lived and worked as a wire editor for the local North Platte newspaper for several freezing months. This is a place where the airport closes for lunch, where the city council prays before each meeting, and where, thanks to lack of demand, relatively large houses rent for a mere four hundred dollars per month. Of course, the garage door blew off during a thunderous windstorm, but the rent was still pretty great. I used to crack that the town's name was painted on the water towers so that the citizenry could check on how to spell it. After putting the paper to bed each night, my coworkers and I would skid over the frozen ice to Doris's Tavern and slam down two-dollar drinks (payable by check if necessary) before last call. Then I'd drive home drunk, watch the Farm Report, and sleep 'til noon. A lousy, lousy town? Yes.

—*Allison Landa*

WISHFUL THINKING BY THE CHAMBER OF COMMERCE

- "Nebraska is the most economical travel destination."
- "Come on in to North Platte! . . . Where living is as comfortable and cozy as an old, easy chair."

PERFECTLY ILLUSTRATIVE HEADLINES FROM
THE NORTH PLATTE BULLETIN

- "Bonus Offered for Aluminum Cans"
- "Council Approves Fight in Ring, Not Bar"
- "Death on the Rails More Mysterious Than It First Appeared"
- "Becky Leet Wins RSVP Quilt"

This might as well be every crappy corner in south Philly.

Philadelphia, PA

The City of Brotherly Love
Philly

Population: 1,517,550
Unemployment: 6.1%
Median Household Income: $30,746
Violent Crime Rate: 1604.5
Climate: Frustrated and somewhat aggressive
Pat's or Geno's: Pat's

Ideal for: South Jersey Ex-pats, The Morbidly Obese, Corrupt Politicians, Gays Deceived by the *Real World* into Thinking This is the San Fran of the East, Forty-Year-Old Italians Still Living with Their Parents, Gangsta Wannabes, Desperate/Violent Sports Fans

Cultural Highlights: Watching the Eagles Blow the Big Game, Eating Cheesesteaks at 3:00 a.m., *Rocky*, LOVE Park, Mummers, the Art Museum Steps (As Opposed to the Actual Art Inside), Melted Cheese, "E-A-G-L-E-S!!!" Chants, Firebombs, Ben Franklin, The Liberty Bell

Philadelphia doesn't seem so bad at first. But the longer you stay, slowly but steadily its shortcomings begin to mount, until they become the source of great angst and frustration. Especially perplexing is the fact that, though New York City beckons from a mere hour and a half straight up the New Jersey Turnpike, people continue to live in Philadelphia. It simply boggles the mind. And so Philly suffers not only for its stubborn reluctance to get its shit together, but by comparison, as well. It's virtually impossible to leave New York, drive to Philly, and not begin immediately wondering, "Where'd everything go?" Philadelphia feels slightly off, as if there exists some collective desire to remain second-rate. The sports teams are abysmal, the people unambitious, the arts scene barely functional, the subway ill-conceived. Even the Liberty Bell has a gigantic crack in it.

Quotes

Philadelphia is by far the worst place I've ever lived. As a widely traveled person who has lived in more than a few major metropolises—Sao Paolo, Madrid, Boston, New York—I rue the day I moved to Philadelphia. Indeed, I count my tenure in the "City of Brotherly Love" as a most lackluster experience. There is absolutely no glam, no good weather, no friendliness, and even though the last twenty years has brought a boom to the restaurant business, there is no attractive place to get an affordable meal.

When did it all go wrong? The very day I drove down from Boston to look for an apartment. The mercury climbed well into the nineties and didn't budge for the next three months. The humidity is such that, in Philly in the summer, you sweat even in the shower. The heat is inescapable and even the rodents are driven from their burrows. I lived for three months with a dead rat decomposing in the front yard next door. Dog walkers allow their pets to relieve themselves wherever and you can't walk down the streets without having to maneuver through an obstacle course of feces, trash, and filth. The pollution is some of the worst in the country, and we have the heavy industry along the Delaware River in conjunction with huge refineries such as the infamous Motiva to thank for the epidemic of asthma that ravages young and old alike. No one can take a clean breath around here. The stench is wretched. And if you like sun and blue skies, well then, you must pick yourself up and move to California because we Philadelphians can count the number of sunny days in a given season on one hand.

Philadelphia has also been named one of the fattest cities in the world. I don't mind a little chubbiness, but I do mind the overall lack of the finer things in life. Take wine, for example, which is available in state-approved stores only, where the prices are steep, the selection limited, and they keep the better bottles under lock and key. Did I mention that you can only buy beer by the case?

Corruption, sluggish employment, sky-high taxes, and violence and criminality make Philadelphia even less appealing. Philadelphia landlords are some of the meanest and the most negligent in the nation. We paid New York City prices to live in a firetrap with no heat in the winter, no air-conditioning in the summer, and where the landlord raised the rent on us every six months. When the frat boys moved in down the hall, we finally felt that we had had enough and moved out to the suburbs.

And where is the love? I have never lived among such contentious people in my life. I have been yelled at by caffeine-crazed drivers, by cell-phone toting mothers, and by hostile neighbors. Once, in Bed Bath & Beyond,

I was chatting with a co-shopper when all of a sudden an elderly man shouted: "Would you just shut up!" And I am not alone in having been the victim of this kind of abuse. A pregnant friend of mine was reduced to tears in Whole Foods by a woman who dressed her down for getting into the express line with too many items. They say that Philadelphia is a city founded on Quaker values, but you could have fooled me.

—*Kathryn A. Kopple*

To really get to the heart of Philadelphia, you must understand the environmental influences that have, over the years, formed the psyche of the average Philadelphian. We are A-holes, plain and simple, united against the world. Philly sticks together like un-oiled South Philly pasta. We are a city with an inferiority complex, stuck between New York City and Washington, D.C. We are a city that has fought to keep hold of a fleeting identity. D.C. stole our "Capitol" title. New York is the hub of culture and hipness. What do we have? Cheesesteaks.

—*Peter R. Geyelin*

The Town That Never Quite Gets It Right—only in Philadelphia is it possible to have a waterfront so disconnected from the city that the only thing you can build there is (duh) a shipbuilding company. After the tragic closing of LOVE Park to the international skateboarding community, DC Shoes offered Philadelphia one million dollars to reopen the park to skaters. Philadelphia officials denied the gift, deciding instead that the park is better served by businesspeople on their lunch hour and homeless people the other twenty-three. Philadelphia's shot at superstardom on MTV's *The Real World* was almost cut short by the labor unions, who felt it was their right to work on the house construction. After long hours of deliberation, MTV and Philadelphia came to an agreement and produced the most boring *Real World* in the series' history, complete with the ugliest cast.

—*Jim Marchese*

LOCAL CUISINE

Despite its shortcomings, Philadelphia has cornered the market on delectable native fare. A junk food lover's paradise, the city is renowned the world over for the following contributions to the American palate:

Cheesesteaks: A point of local passion, pride, and much debate, authentic Philly cheesesteaks require the use of a hoagie roll (baked in Philadelphia), Cheez Wiz (provolone or American being also acceptable), and fried rib eye. Onions and mushrooms are optional.

Hoagies: The local term for a submarine (or, heaven forbid, grinder) sandwich, hoagies usually involve plentiful amounts of Italian cold cuts and should only be ordered from authentic, old-school delis such as Primo's.

Scrapple: This hardcore Pennsylvania meat product consists of cornmeal mashed together with leftover pig parts, fried, then sliced.

Water Ice: Frozen, flavored ice product served in a small cup and eaten with a wooden spoon.

Philadelphia Soft Pretzels: Unbelievably good, dense, salty pretzels usually sold in unmarked brown paper bags. Great at any temperature, those in the know make early morning trips to the pretzel factory in order to score a batch straight from the oven.

Tastykake: Purveyor of cakes, cookies, and other sweets, Tastykake is the Cadillac of mass produced baked goods. The butterscotch krimpet is its rightful flagship.

GREAT SEMIRECENT MOMENTS IN PHILADELPHIA SPORTS HISTORY (ABRIDGED)

- **1968**—Santa Claus is booed and mercilessly pelted with snowballs during halftime of an Eagles game. Stadium officials help him off the field.
- **Various Years**—Following the annual Easter egg hunt at Veteran's Stadium, fans boo children who find no eggs.

- **1994**—Phillies closer Mitch Williams bolts town under a barrage of death threats following his serving up a meatball to Joe Carter in Game Six of the World Series.
- **1999**—Eagles fans enthusiastically jeer Dallas Cowboys wide receiver Michael Irvin as he lay writhing on the turf, having just suffered a career-ending neck injury.
- **1999**—St. Louis Cardinals outfielder JD Drew, admittedly one of the great Phillies villains, is pelted with D batteries from the stands.
- **1999**—Matthew Scott, first hand transplant recipient in the United States, is booed after bouncing the ceremonial first pitch to the plate before the Phillies' home opener. And yes, he threw it with the transplanted hand.
- **2005**—In true Live 8 spirit, Phillies reserve outfielder Jason Michaels celebrates the day's activities by brawling with a uniformed police officer at 3 a.m.

From this height, Quartzsite only appears marginally terrible.

Quartzsite, AZ

Rock and Gem Capital of the World

Population: 3,354
Median Household Income: $23,053
Ideal for: RV People, Geology Nuts, Off-roaders, Fossil Hunters
Cultural Highlights: Mineral Crystallization, Trailer Parks, Navajo Rugs, Assorted Junk

If you're a big, big fan of rocks (and who isn't?), Quartzsite, Arizona, is no doubt high on your list of travel destinations. Alternately described as a rock hunter's paradise, an RV owner's mecca, and a bad idea for anyone under the age of seventy-five, this former stagecoach station and Indian fightin' fort has refashioned itself into one of the least likely tourist traps in America. Over *one million* people make their way to Quartzsite annually, most during the winter months of January and February, when the world's biggest swap meet blooms in the desert, along with myriad other shows and activities geared mostly toward the geological and mobile-home enthusiast. It's said that some of the bigger shows, such as the Main Event and the Tyson Wells, can take days to fully experience. Yes, days.

During the summer, when the temperature soars and tourists flee, Quartzsite reverts back to the sleepy, dusty, dismal desert town it actually is. Unless your car breaks down, keep driving. It's only two hours to Phoenix.

Quotes

The worst town I ever drove through is Quartzsite, Arizona. I stopped because I had to pee and it was basically the last stop before Phoenix. This place looked like it was something out of *Ghost Town Weekly*. There was hardly anyone around except for a few stray dogs. Actual tumbleweeds passed by. The town's biggest claims to fame are rock and gem shows, a few swimming pools (privately available to the mobile home park residents who live there), and large influxes of RVing snowbirds, therefore making it difficult to give an actual account of the population. I don't know what's so attractive about Quartzsite . . . possibly it's the entertainment value of seeing Billy Bob's toothless grin as he kicks back at the local gas station or watching the tumbleweeds blow through the dust. Sure, they've acquired the metropolitan effects of a Dairy Queen and Love's Truck Stop. But it's still a dusty town full of rock collectors and oldtimers who hang tires on chain-link fences so that their old Ford pickups won't ruin the homestead or head out on the open road by themselves. If you are an East Coaster, it's worth the drive to Phoenix just to see this place. Truly unbelievable.

—*Heidi Ollman*

CHECK IT OUT!

In addition to dust, gems, and bad fashion, Quartzsite is home to one of the most unusual monuments in the United States, the Grave of Hi Jolly. Consisting of a copper camel perched atop a stone pyramid, the memorial is meant to commemorate the short-lived U.S. Camel Corps. Named for lead camel driver Hadji Ali, "Hi Jolly" is based on the bastardization of his Syrian name, which proved much too difficult for the local desert folk to wrap their tongues around.

WISHFUL THINKING BY THE CHAMBER OF COMMERCE

"Quartzite, Arizona: Where Every Day is a Weekend."

Rock Springs: a bunch of crap in the desert.

Rock Springs, WY

Gateway to the West

Population: 18,708
Median Household Income: $42,584
Ideal for: Meth Heads, Oil Pumpin' Cowboys, Ambitionless White Trash
Cultural Highlights: Dinosaur Bones, Pawnshops, Ecological Rape, Meth, Monotony

This old mining town, which began life as a stopover on the Overland Stage Route, continues to function as something of a crossroads. Freight trains barrel through and truckers pull off the road for some coffee and a spot of grease, while the coal-burning power plant churns away right smack up against the Red Desert, a pristine and untamed wilderness apparently begging to be thoroughly plundered for its natural gas deposits. Today's conflict between environmentalists and the oil and gas industry hearkens back to those bygone days when white miners clashed with their Chinese counterparts over wages. This ended with the latter being massacred by the hundreds, their nascent Chinatown burned to the ground (the destruction was so total that you still can't find decent ethnic food in Rock Springs). Who'll win this latest skirmish is anyone's guess, but the smart money isn't on the tree huggers.

Quotes

People enter Rock Springs for two reasons: either to drill in the Red Desert (one of the country's most fragile ecosystems) or to score some homemade methamphetamine. It's the meth capital of the world. Wyoming's taxpayers pay a shitload of money to have inmates fitted for dentures because the meth rots their teeth out. Everybody there sucks ass. It feels almost like every person in the town is either a drunk angry red-neck or a crack head.

—*Matt Naughton*

It seems to be a mining town. . . . It seems to be the Wild and Woolly West with a vengeance.

—*Jack London, 1894*

A RECIPE FOR SUCCESS!

Opportunity knocks in Rock Springs, where it's easy for anyone to make a decent living, white trash included. Don't even bother with that high school diploma (most locals don't). All that's required is dedication, a little chutzpah, and the following household ingredients (http://www.streetdrugs.org/methlabs2.htm):

- Alcohol (Isopropyl or rubbing alcohol)
- Toluene (brake cleaner)
- Ether (engine starter)
- Sulfuric Acid (drain cleaner)
- Red Phosphorus (matches/road flares)
- Salt (table/rock)
- Iodine (teat dip or flakes/crystal)
- Lithium (batteries)
- Trichloroethane (gun scrubber)
- MSM (cutting agent)

- Sodium Metal
- Methanol/Alcohol (gasoline additives)
- Muriatic Acid
- Anhydrous Ammonia (farm fertilizer)
- Sodium Hydroxide (lye)
- Pseudoephedrine (cold tablets)
- Ephedrine (cold tablets)
- Acetone
- Cat Litter

Next, simply follow the instructions available via simple Google search, implement a distribution system, and voila! Your crank will be on the streets of Rock Springs in no time.

IT HAPPENED HERE!

The outlaw Robert LeRoy Parker, better known as Butch Cassidy, earned the nickname "Butch" while employed as a butcher in Rock Springs. At the time, he was on a break from his more lucrative career in horse theft and train robbery.

ROUND UP THE POSSE

Just as posses once helped tame the wilder aspects of the Wild West, a loose coalition of forces has banded together to help defeat the scourge of Big

Oil and Gas. Those currently patrolling Rock Springs include:

- The Biodiversity Conservation Alliance
- The Wyoming Outdoor Council
- The Sierra Club
- The National Wildlife Federation
- The Wyoming Wildlife Federation
- The Wilderness Society

Citizens are urged to write their congressman in lieu of taking to the streets with rifles and hangin' rope.

Salt Lake City, UT

Crossroads of the West

Population: 181,743
African American Percent of Population: 1.97%
Median Household Income: $36,944
Violent Crime Rate: 710.1
Climate: Extremely conservative
Estimated Wives Per Household: 3.6
Ideal for: Jesus, Whites, Men Named Ezekiel,
    Patriarchs, Steve Young, Toeheads, Blue-Haired
    Bouffants, Laura Ashley Clones, Forty-Year-Old
    Virgins, Polygamists, Family Historians

Cultural Highlights: Polygamy, Prepubescent Wives, Tithing, Choral Music, Karl Malone, Touring Theatre, The Osmonds, Mormon Conferences/Tabernacle Choir, Monster Trucks, Dragging State Street, Censored Films, Shakespeare Festivals, Arts and Crafts, Stepford Smiles

Salt Lake City is clean, wholesome, and self-contained. It boasts a perfectly charming downtown, brimming with wide boulevards and framed by nearby, snow-capped mountains. Its citizens are polite, hospitable, and eager to please. Instead of drinking coffee or smoking cigarettes, the locals busy themselves passing out religious literature and cajoling tourists into taking a peek at one or another church-related curios. Everything is just so . . . nice. Like vanilla ice cream or a boxful of puppies. Salt Lake City is a Hallmark store writ large. In other words, it's exactly what you don't want in a major metropolitan center.

Still, the area does admittedly possess some natural beauty and some supposedly outstanding skiing, hiking, and mountain biking. If dodging Mormons can also be considered a physical activity, then Salt Lake City isn't a bad place to get some exercise in. And if culture, nightlife, and socializing aren't your thing, Salt Lake City might be worth a look.

Quotes

It's full of Mormons, one of the most loathsome cults in the panoply of superstitions that plagues this land.

—*Matthew Shultz*

Depending on who you talk to, it's colloquially referred to as either Shit Lake City or Salt Lake Shitty. It has to be the only town where The Church built itself the highest building and then cajoled the state congress into passing legislation prohibiting other structures from going higher up. They can also purchase a section of Main Street, turn it into a "public park," then regulate people's behavior by prohibiting smoking and swearing in the park.

Two of the city's gay bars, the Sun and the Deer Hunter, suffered God's wrath, the first falling under a tornado that hit SLC back in 2001 and the second a mysterious fire. And, of course, the classic: they charge you a membership fee to enter a club, then only serve alcohol containing 3.2 percent of the good stuff. Makes you want to cry sometimes. At least the altitude is high enough that you still get tanked . . . if you go for a run directly afterward.

—*RJ*

If this is God's Kingdom on Earth, I'd hate to see the real thing.

—*Lara Turner*

IT HAPPENED HERE!

In 1999, incensed that Des Moines, Iowa, had dared consume more Jell-O brand gelatin, the citizens of Salt Lake City rallied to reclaim the number-one position in terms of national per-capita Jell-O consumption. Said local chef Scott Blackerby, "Jell-O is as much a part of Utah as the Great Salt Lake, our world famous powder skiing, and our scenic national parks." (http://saltlakecity.about.com/cs/regionalfood/1/aajelloofficial.htm)

MORMON 101

Everyone knows that Mormons are a goofy lot. But just how goofy? Consider the following:

- Much of the religion's origin story is concerned with the exploits of a magical, talking hat.
- People of color, thought marked as punishment for their sins, were unable to occupy the priesthood until 1978, when the Church received a brand-new revelation from God and reversed this decree. Just in the knick of time, it turned out, as the institution was being threatened with losing its tax-exempt status if changes weren't made.
- Mormons believe that not only was God once a man, but an alien, as well. In fact, he currently re-

sides on a distant planet beside a star called Kolob.

- The faith's founder and first prophet, Joseph Smith, Jr., is thought to have concurrently enjoyed the company of somewhere between thirty and forty wives.

- Eschewing boxers *and* briefs, Mormons must wear a mysterious form of underwear referred to as "the Garment." Essentially a cross between long johns and old-fashioned swim trunks, the Garment's expansive acreage promotes modesty and is thought by some wearers to provide supernatural powers of protection.

Seattle's overrated skyline.

Seattle, WA

The Emerald City

Population: 569,000
Median Household Income: $45,567
Violent Crime Rate: 767.3
Climate: Overcast and overcaffeinated
Ideal for: Liberals, Supposed Liberals, the Humorless, Burned Out Actual Hippies, Bright Eyed Neo-Hippies, Enlightened Conservatives, Microsoft Millionaires, Baristas, Fish Tossers, Tourists, Dwindling Natives

Cultural Highlights: Pike Place Market, the Space Needle, Coffee, Pioneer Square Violence, Fusion Food, SUVs, Political Correctness, Disney World-esque Public Transportation, Microbrews, Overpriced Everything, Rain

Seattle? But doesn't everyone love Seattle, what with all its cute little cafés, its flying fish, its lovely coastline, its tons of hippies? Well, maybe not the hippies. But still, Seattle's great, isn't it? Upon closer examination, "overrated" might be a more apt description.

Quotes

Seattle used to be a relatively nice place to live until it started believing its own hype. There is no realism left, only pretension. It's a rudderless environment built upon make-believe. I can put up with a lot, but don't bullshit me.

Used to be, if you thought of Seattle, you thought of Boeing—maybe a salmon or two, a faint vision of mountains tumbling down to deep bays, but mostly Boeing. Today, there's much, much more. More corruption. More mediocrity. More mirthless, self-important dogma. More insipid *Frasier* reruns.

Seattleites are still convinced Clinton's in the White House and Sam is still sleepless in Seattle. Like Dorothy in *The Wizard of Oz,* my neighbors believe that if you say something over and over, it will become true. Small wonder this place is nicknamed the Emerald City. Take away the delusions and you'll find a small town without the grace and humor of small-town folk, a business center succeeding despite the worst motives, a city whose public morality belongs in a cesspool.

Back to the hype: the place used to have hard hands and broad shoulders. It cut down big trees, launched big ships, caught big fish, built big airplanes—and did it all with a self-deprecating sense of humor. That was before Bill Gates taught the city to make money through mediocrity, before the city identified itself with brown sugar water, and before Boeing forgot how to make jets.

When one of your leading citizens rose to prominence for convincing people to pay $2.50 for a 50-cent cup of coffee, earning a modest, honest living loses quite a bit of its appeal. The city begins to rot from the core. University of Washington physicians admitted to stealing from the poor and the university paid a $35 million fine. Boeing executives went to prison for bribery. Sure, Puget Sound and the Cascade Mountains still define Seattle visually, but the people have adopted a permanent case of adolescent insecurity. Seattle is preening and self-congratulatory, utterly afraid the charade will be exposed.

The newspapers themselves have lost touch with what

made this community great. The new Seattleites have taken the velvet glove of Scandinavian liberalism and transmuted it into Titoism circa 1971, except everyone wants to be a member of the politburo. There's no laughter in Seattle, only edicts handed down by apparatchiks of suffocating solemnity. The far left acts amazingly like the far right: they talk of love but hate all nonbelievers. The agony and anger after George W. Bush's election in 2004 was palpable. Our local public radio station, showing its usual lack of objectivity, opened a call-in show the day after with a recording of a saloon chanteuse threatening suicide. The rest of the hour was consumed by lefties questioning the morals and intellect of those on the prevailing side—precisely the type of bloviating you'd expect from Rush Limbaugh.

Bill Gates accomplished his coup by subsuming and silencing competitors, through business tactics that border on unethical, and with a business model he describes as evolution, not revolution. At least his foundation does noble work. Bill's coconspirator, Paul Allen, spends his money on the adolescent joys of rock 'n' roll, sports, and rocket ships. For his Experience Music Project rock museum, Allen hired internationally renowned architect Frank Gehry, who produced a building so ghastly that it can be considered only as a joke on the rubes, rich and poor, of Seattle. The building looks like a very large, freshly butchered beef heart sprawled in great flaccidity near the Space Needle.

Very few of Seattle's new plutocracy have embraced the arts. The symphony is good, but not world-class. And what major city can take its place in the artistic firmament without a theater scene? But surely Seattle rocks, right? It does, but with a petulance that's pure Seattle. While Kurt lay cooling on the floor, his blood and brains drying around him, wife Courtney was in L.A. saying Seattle was the best place in the nation to score heroin. No one complains about mainlining smack in the Emerald City, but you might be lynched for lighting up a Marlboro.

Did I mention the traffic? Worst in the nation, say some. Others, the apologists, maintain it's only the fourth-worst. Then there's the price of housing. Want a Brady Bunch split level? Got half a million bucks? Real people can't afford to live in Seattle, yet the biggest newspaper is so stunningly tone-deaf to the Aspenization that it published a how-to section on becoming emotionally attached to your new home.

In Seattle, we never learn and we don't remember. A duchess of this town, if not an actual queen, achieved her regency by funding a foundation that champions environmental causes. Subjects swoon over her philanthropic purity, ignoring the ghastly irony that the money originally came from the very old Seattle pursuit of cutting down every tree in sight.

Not all of Seattle has gone bad. You still see some of the old backbone sticking out, the old toughness, the old tolerance, the old humor. Just don't go to Pike Place Market to find what's real. Some culturally blind civic booster, giddy with hyperbole, proclaimed the market to be "Seattle's soul." Hogwash. It's an amusement park for those fat-of-wallet and easily amused.

—*Don McManman*

I was underwhelmed by Seattle. I think the raves are from people coming from California and the Midwest, oohing and aaahing either over the mountains, the water, or the greenery.

—*Andrew Buckley*

Skid Row, Los Angeles, CA

The Nickel

Population: 7,000 to 8,000 (reports vary)
Unemployment: 100% (give or take)
Median Household Income: N/A (due to lack of households)
Ideal for: Alcoholics, Vagrants, Mission Workers, Gawkers
Cultural Highlights: Single-Room-Occupancy Hotels, Outdoor Living, Cheap Parking, Destitution

Welcome to Los Angeles, where Skid Row is more than just a washed-up metal band. Partially hidden among the toy and flower bargains of downtown's Wholesale District (located east of Main, roughly between Third and Eighth Streets) lurks the country's largest service-dependent ghetto, a literal shantytown seemingly impervious to gentrification and let out to pasture by the city. The very sight of Skid Row is a shock, as this is the sort of thing one imagines does not exist anymore, at least not in a world where Whole Foods stands one block from The Bowery. And yet there it is: an entire district given over to abject poverty, the streets literally lined with tents (actual tents!), cardboard boxes, swirling papers, the detritus of despair. Skid Row is like something out of Dickens or *Taxi Driver* or the BBC World News. It's either of another time or another place, or both. It can't really be just down the street from In-N-Out Burger, can it?

Meanwhile, directly overhead, glistening skyscrapers mock the situation, the people of LA too busy partying in the Hills to give much notice. As is typical of this town, social agenda does not apply to one's own backyard. These are the same folks, after all, who decry the Bush administration's oil policies while refusing to utilize public transportation.

Quotes

Even in daylight, Skid Row feels like a scene out of *Escape from New York*. The inhabitants almost seem blurry. They amble in slow-mo. It's impossible to assess how many of them there are. They're in every nook, every spot you can get your back against. The aimless barely care to step aside and make way for a vehicle. They puff the life out of found butts. They orbit their shopping cart caravan. They stay in the shade. They pass the bottle around, huddled in small groups.

The scene looks like the broken and decrepit skeleton of some lost schoolyard on perpetual recess. An eerie urban playground standing smack in the middle of it all amplifies this. Freshly painted, looking brand-new, the playground is a stark and surreal anomaly. The people fill the sandbox, they crowd the benches, they buzz around and gesticulate in a subdued, almost tribal manner. There are so many of them obscuring the view that if you don't already know it's there, the playground is practically invisible. It looks like they're all packed into a huge green cage.

—*George Griffith*

I take the bus right through Skid Row twice a day. It materializes practically from out of nowhere, and it's always a surprise. You know it's coming, you know what it looks like, and yet it never fails to shock. The bus falls completely silent, people's conversations just trail off . . .

like it's disrespectful or something to small talk your way through Skid Row. Chatting would be like blasting your radio in a funeral procession. Skid Row demands a certain reverence, a certain there-but-for-the-grace-of-God reflection (as if just riding the bus in LA weren't gesture enough). This only lasts a couple of blocks, this eerie silence. The bus pushes its way through the swirling debris, past the rows of tents and cardboard boxes, careful to avoid any wayward derelicts who've wandered drunkenly out into the middle of the street. And then it's gone and things *instantly* revert to normal. Chatter picks up, the driver's radio squawks, you can breathe again. And Skid Row is pretty much forgotten until the next trip, sort of like a bad dream. Which is what Skid Row is.

—*Mike Standlish*

A misleadingly lovely scene from Springfield.

Springfield, MO

Queen City of the Ozarks

Population: 151,580
Median Household Income: $29,563
Climate: Seasonal and hyperconservative
Ideal for: Good Ol' Boys, Rednecks, Donald Rumsfeld, Anti-Semites, Retired Military Personnel (FBI and CIA included)
Cultural Highlights: Lynching, Corruption, Jew-Baiting, Confederate Flags, Methamphetamine, Small-Town Charm

Terrible towns everywhere should take a cue from Springfield, Missouri's PR campaign. For, while chambers of commerce nationwide strain to put a happy spin on even the most dreadful spots, Springfield's public image is truly something to behold. According to the party line, Springfield is a downright utopia of cowboy lore, cappuccino culture, Route 66 Americana, and wholesome Christian values. Naturally, there's a healthy job market, great schools, even a supposedly active arts community. In Springfield, where Union and Confederate soldiers lie buried side by side, even the Civil War feels warm and fuzzy.

Of course, the city's official literature somehow fails to mention Springfield's history of racism, its rampant methamphetamine abuse, its Good Ol' Boy social and political networking, its lackadaisical law enforcement, or even, on a less inflammatory level, its lack of modern urban amenities like major league sports or a subway. Things are not as they appear in Springfield, Missouri. Or, at least things are not as they appear on Springfield, Missouri's Web site.

Quotes

The Ozarks are separated from the outside world by mountainous roads, Civil War resentments, hate groups, fanatical fundamentalism, and righteous paranoia. This isolation has led to a clannish, homogeneous society of insiders who fear, hate, and exclude outsiders, especially minorities. It's ironic that the Ozarks are famous for folksy hospitality, Christian tourism, family values, and peaceful retirement. The hypocrisy of Springfield is epitomized by the fact that it is both the buckle of the Bible Belt and the buckle of the Meth Belt. Springfield is like Miss Piggy—she thinks she's beautiful, but she's a pig.

—*Jeff Biener and Mary Meriam, ozarkopathy.org*

SPRINGFIELD: WHERE DRUGS AND RACISM COLLIDE!

Tom McNamara, of the Southern Illinois Enforcement Group (or SIEG, no pun intended), believes the current Midwestern meth crisis can be traced to one man, a Springfield native, who began producing the drug after returning from a West Coast trip. Of course, this being Springfield, Missouri, the perpetrator's research quickly led him to the so-called "Nazi recipe" for meth production, a method thought to have originated in Nazi Germany.

IT HAPPENED HERE!

Wild Bill Hickock kicked off the Wild West on July 21, 1865, gunning down Dave Tutt over a gambling dispute in the town square.

A DEMOGRAPHIC NOTE

African Americans make up roughly 4 percent of Springfield's population. The number has remained low since 1906, when fully one-third of Springfield's black residents fled the city in a single week, following the public lynching of three African Americans in the town square.

COMMUNITY ORGANIZATIONS

Visitors to Springfield, especially those considering a move to the area, may want to check out one or more of the following groups, all of whom help give Springfield its special flair and are a testament to the city's strong sense of charity and community.

- **Springfield Hospitality Club**—Helps new residents become familiar with their community through monthly luncheons and social activity groups.
- **Hammerskin Nation**—The most violent and best-organized neo-Nazi skinhead group in the United States (according to the Anti-Defamation League).
- **Springfield Rotary Club**—The oldest club in the Ozarks, this community-minded group makes volunteer work its priority.

- **Creativity Movement**—Dedicated to the Survival, Expansion, and Advancement of the White Race.
- **United Way of the Ozarks**—Exemplars of community service, the United Way is dedicated to addressing the full range of Springfield's human needs.

St. Cloud, MN

Granite City

Population: 59,107
Median Household Income: $37,346
Ideal for: Dazed and Ill-Prepared College Students,
   Pedantic and Insecure Faculty, University
   Bureaucrats, Obese Buffet Grazers, Downtown
   Crack Heads, Lutherans, Catholics, Mall Rats
Cultural Highlights: The Public Library, Country-Style
   Buffet, Hockey, Frozen Pizza, Arby's, Movie
   Theater, Ice Fishing, Church, The Mall, Drinking,
   Dairy Queen, Breweries/Sports Bars

St. Cloud, Minnesota, considers itself a college town, which might come as some surprise to anyone who's set foot in, say, Boston, Massachusetts, Austin, Texas, or Seattle, Washington. Yes, St. Cloud State University, St. Cloud Technical College, and several other supposed institutes of higher learning are sprinkled about, but the term "college town" usually implies the existence of a vibrant arts scene, a truly intellectual (and often progressive) perspective, and world-class social options (cuisine, cinema, music, theater, galleries, museums, that sort of thing).

St. Cloud, on the other hand, is highlighted by a miniature circus, a couple of public gardens, designer fire hydrants, and the Stearns History Museum, where visitors may thrill to the history of granite.

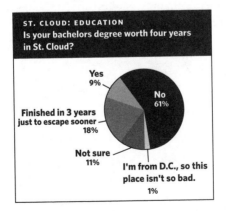

ST. CLOUD: EDUCATION
Is your bachelors degree worth four years in St. Cloud?

Yes
9%

No
61%

Finished in 3 years just to escape sooner
18%

Not sure
11%

I'm from D.C., so this place isn't so bad.
1%

Quotes

Just about the most joyless and depressing university town imaginable. If its endless below-zero winter doesn't kill you, its soul-killing culture of sheer hopelessness surely will. Besides watching college hockey, residents seem to placate their misery with quite possibly the highest number of Arby's per capita and the longest frozen pizza grocery aisles in the nation.

The people are somber and petty and make no effort to beautify their city architecturally. It should be a decent place based on its size and the university, plus two good catholic colleges nearby. But since the weather tries to kill you most of the time, why bother going outside unless it's for a dutiful trip to the family picnic or pool party? There's one nice theater downtown, which is struggling, and some events at the colleges. But outside of that, there's almost no culture at all. And it's the largest city in central Minnesota.

In the summer, when most students and faculty leave, the place can feel like a ghost town. Then you're even more likely to encounter the country bumpkins from Lake Wobegon who drive in to the hellish, never-ending strip-mall drag for supplies. There's an old downtown area close to the university that could be charming if it weren't depressed from so much strip-mall competition. There could be a charming pedestrian atmosphere, but why spend time walking when you've got a climate-controlled vehicle? Plus, since 50 percent of the people are obese, just moving around outside is a heroic feat. I don't know how those people manage to get up in the morning. I guess religion helps since most are churchgoers.

Basically, people constantly eat bad food at buffet-style restaurants and watch themselves get fat. I don't think there are more than five restaurants that don't offer some buffet garbage option, which immediately becomes the most popular attraction. Dieting and health food have little place here. A Wild Oats market opened and only lasted a year.

—*Dave McCoy*

ST. CLOUD'S ETHNIC DIVERSITY

St. Cloud is truly a melting pot of different races and cultures, as attested to by the area's several Mexican restaurants. With demographics like these, it's a virtual Ellis Island around here.

- White—95.03%
- Asian—2.42%
- Black—1.63%
- American Indian—0.86%
- Hispanic—0.87%
- Other—0.24%

DONNA REYNOLDS

Thank God for cheap alcohol.

Syracuse, NY

Salt City

Population: 147,306
Median Household Income: $25,000
Violent Crime Rate: 944.3
Ideal for: Coeds on the Walk of Shame, Token Black Athletes, Middle Management Thugs, Permanently Babyfat Undergrads, Professors Too Lazy to Actually Be Lechers, Drug-Dealing Convenience Store Owners, People Who Won't Venture Downtown, Mullet-Sportin' Townies

Cultural Highlights: Precipitation, Shopping at the Carousel Center, SU Basketball, Fishing in Toxic Waters, Cutting Off Pedestrians, Driving Half an Hour Each Way to Rent a Movie, Dreaming of Life in Rochester, Hooter's, The Dream Girls' Gentleman's Club

The country's greatest rate of annual snowfall, roving packs of drunk Frat Boys, plus the troubling decline of local manufacturing help make Syracuse the crown jewel of that impressive collection of horrible midsize cities known as Western New York.

Quotes

Let me break Syracuse down for you in all its repulsive glory:

- *Multiple* locations regularly sell past-date meat and dairy. In fact, there's an entire store devoted to out-of-date meat, which is located, naturally, in the Farmer's Market. Even the health food co-op sells out-of-date milk, yogurt, and cheese (But, hey, when they notice it's past-date, they give you 50 cents off. What a deal!). If you want your out-of-date meat butchered in front of you by someone who doesn't wear gloves to cover his bloody, bloody hands, then Syracuse has that, too!

- The public transportation system was apparently designed to suit the memory limitations of a Commode 64. Literally every bus in the city has to pass through the same central point in order to get to another side of the city—at which central point each bus inevitably stops and waits for an interminable period. Not only is the process slow and inefficient, but it fosters a culture of hustlers and petty crime.

- The city's main natural attraction, Lake Onondaga, is considered the most polluted lake in the country, yet people still sail and fish there. Hundreds of thousands of pounds of mercury have been dumped in the lake, and 20 percent of its source water is processed waste. There's even an eighty-four-acre section comprised of pure waste.

- Syracuse University manages to combine the dumb-fucks-rule culture of a football-mad party school with the privilege-heavy attitude of an Ivy League institution. Jocks and business types run the place, the student newspaper is involved in a different "Hey, don't be so touchy you blacks, it's only a joke" controversy pretty much every semester, and the number of trees on the main campus can be counted on one hand.

- The *Syracuse New Times* (the weekly alternative paper) is, in a word, unreadable. The articles on local politics are long, long, long and full of the worst, nonacademic writing in the country. The writer responsible for something like half to two-thirds of the cover stories thinks introductory phrases are obligatory and does not know the meaning of the term *active verb*.

- A shopping mall is considered to be the economic center of the city. It is literally regarded as a shining beacon of Syracuse's future growth and flourishing. Of course, it's surrounded by hazardous waste sites.
- Syracuse is as segregated as a modern city can be.
- Legend has it that the University is built on a Native American burial ground, which possibly accounts for the area's unmistakably empty and cursed atmosphere.
- The weather, of course, is atrocious, with mountains of snow and an incredibly high percentage of depressingly overcast and rainy days.
- Everyone in Syracuse possesses the same "fuck you" attitude. Bitter screaming over parking spaces, to cite but one example, is the norm.

—*David Ramm*

Syracuse is the greyest place on earth.

—*Nicolette*

Perhaps, to be fair, I should preface my account with insight into my roots: naïve graduate of a Midwestern, private, primarily Caucasian high school. I would like readers to entertain the possibility that my perception of Syracuse as a postapocalyptic, god-forsaken land is the result of skewed vision. In reality though, I fear this *is* the true Syracuse: the butt hole of New York State.

The day my mother drove me across the Syracuse city limits, I almost succumbed to hysteria. Before me appeared a city where one would sooner dispose of toxic waste or incriminating evidence than send their academic superstar. The skyline was littered with abandoned industrial plants and operational ones still billowing noxious, black clouds into the air. Homeless people stood perched at *every* streetlight, ready to swoop down upon idle cars or Prada purses. The city was devoid of color or any signs of potential happiness or excitement to be had . . . well, except for endless billboards advertising alcohol. The restaurants available for patronage were chains spawned in the eighties that had long ago ceased to exist in more major, metropolitan areas (I had only heard of the "Ground Round" in legend until I dined there one typical Syracuse evening).

The climate is subarctic blizzard snowstorm hell . . . and yes, that is an official climate category. I am still astonished that the freshman welcome packet did not come complete with personal snow rescue dog. I would have gladly taken Mushing 101 if it meant learning to walk in heels in October without breaking my neck on black ice.

University students were susceptible to late-night batterings from local mobs. The culture clash between student and townie was blatantly obvious, as one trip to the Carousel Mall could easily illustrate. Throughout my four years there and to this day, I continually wonder how residents find reason to wake in the morning, to breathe, to brush their hair. Someone must be slipping Red Bull into the water supply.

—*Krissi S.*

Romance, Tulsa style.

Tulsa, OK

Former Oil Capital of the World

Population: 393,049
Median Household Income: $35,316
Violent Crime Rate: 1162.1
Tell-Tale Sign That Tulsa Surely Sucks: "Tulsa is a wonderful place to live, work, raise children, and worship."—Tulsa.com
Ideal for: Super Christians, Fetuses, NRA Cardholders, Fat Beer-Guzzling Truck Drivers, Soft-Spoken Bible Peddlers, Used Car Salesmen Turned Ministers (or Vice Versa), Pushy Southern Baptists, Drag Queens

Once those pesky Indians had been dealt with, Tulsa blossomed into the cattle drivin', oil pumpin' boomtown it still pretends to be. Though similarly dreadful Houston, Texas, now holds the heavyweight Oil Capital of the World title, Tulsa's towering Golden Driller statue continues to function as the enduring, if somewhat desperate, symbol of the city, a Statue of Liberty for the crude oil set. Waning industry aside, modern Tulsa is noted for its rental car companies, Indian casinos, extreme weather, and suspiciously low cost of living. A strong sense of history pervades much of the Tulsan experience, to the extent that locals seem utterly reluctant and practically unable to move forward. Tulsa retains a vibrant link to the past through its wonderful collection of structures dating from the 1930s and '40s, as well as through the many deceased citizens raised from the dead by local evangelist Oral Roberts.

Quotes

Tulsa is the most horrible, depressing city to pass through on a Greyhound bus.

—Anne

Oklahoma—erk! I hate that place. . . . Ever been to Tulsa? Last time I drove through I said I'd never set foot in the state again. No matter where I was going, I'd find a way to avoid Oklahoma in its entirety. Tulsa is overwhelmingly boring, flat, and uninteresting to look at. It has a big major toll road going through it, which is the only reason people care or realize that it's there. Well, that and the fact that the biggest McDonald's in the United States is right outside of town, complete with a gift shop. It hovers over the toll road so you can watch the cars go by as you eat. You can see people in town, but there really isn't much of a metropolis, so you wonder where all these cars are going. Probably an Indian casino.

—Beth Dowell

By 1905, Tulsa had earned the name "Oil Capital of the World" for its fortuitous resource. Based on the volume of incredible Art Deco architecture downtown, this fortune must have been going strong well into the 1940s. However, being landlocked and supported mainly by the finite resource of petroleum and the extremely feeble

Arkansas River, it seems that fortune has hit Tulsa like the proverbial tornado, one that sadly may be on its inevitable retreat. Tulsa's economy is now supported mainly by companies whose futures are unstable at best. Parts of downtown are left for decay, with echoes of bustling activity from more prosperous times haunting the streets.

A few tenacious people around Tulsa continually make valiant efforts to create downtown nightlife, but many of these places have traded owners, fallen into decline, or been vacated. Only the hardier restaurants, clubs, and galleries have survived. Having lived there for the better part of fourteen years, I have a soft spot for these fledgling attempts at creating a cultural identity. But without a huge influx of supporters, a substantial rise in the economy, or the installation of a major public university, I fear, at least for the time being, that downtown nightlife is in for a slow, painful decline.

Uptown, on the other hand, is filling up with Starbucks, Walgreens, franchise restaurants, and retail stores. While that's encouraging for the economy, it's also a little disheartening, because it's becoming Everytown, America, with people living in McMansions and driving vehicles that chug gas in outrageous quantities, in complete disregard for the now-struggling resource that once made Tulsa famous. It seems what used to make Tulsa a unique place to live: the impressive Art Deco architecture, the Native American history, the novelty that cowboys once ruled the land, is now fading into the neon light of the Krispy Kremes and Bank of Americas.

—Rebecca

Tulsans think the world revolves around them, and if anything is done to challenge them they are as close-minded as one would expect any Podunk backwater to be. My advice to anyone thinking of moving to Tulsa or Oklahoma is *do not do it*. The town is dying, the state is backward, and a lot of the people are the self-righteous narrow-minded clods one would expect.

—The Tulsan

A BRIEF DISSENTING OPINION

Compared to Oklahoma City, Tulsa is heaven.

—Alan Stanwick

Race riots not pictured.

Virginia Beach, VA

Population: 425,257
Median Household Income: $48,705
Climate: Hot and rowdy
Ideal for: Guys in Cutoffs, College Drunks Hoping
Girls Gone Wild Makes a Pit Stop, Hookers with
Nice Tans, Retirees, The Military, Surfers
Cultural Highlights: Disgusting Hotel Rooms, Traffic,
Large Crowds, Overpriced Parking, Litter, Palpable
Police Presence, Hurricanes, Greekfest Riots,
Alcohol, Mount Trashmore, Boardwalk Kitsch, Golf

Like many East Coast shore towns, Virginia Beach has a split personality. In the off-season, when it's cool, calm, and sleepy, one might actually appreciate its natural beauty, its sprawling beaches, world-famous golf course, and extensive parkland. Also noteworthy is the fact that Virginia Beach stands adjacent to one of the Seven Engineering Wonders of the World, namely the twenty-three-mile long Chesapeake Bay Bridge-Tunnel. So that's kind of cool.

And then comes summer, when Virginia Beach's seaside tranquility is shattered by what might be the most thick and hideous concentration of overheated collegiate sexuality this side of MTV's *Spring Break*. It's like someone filled a dirty bomb with obnoxious frat guys and set it off in the middle of the boardwalk. And remember, this is the South, where people take things like Greek Life and racial stereotypes quite seriously, to the extent that in addition to the expected rowdiness, binge drinking, homoerotic male bonding, and aggressive fondling, Virginia Beach also features riots, looting, and violence, as locals clash with visitors during Beach Week.

Quotes

Virginia Beach is a watered-down, mid-Atlantic version of the skuzzy beach town in *The Lost Boys* (only minus Jami Gertz). If you're looking to spend your one and only work-free week of the summer sardined into a crowd of overweight bickering families wearing incomprehensibly juvenile T-shirts (such as "My Other Wife is J-Lo," "I'm With Stoopid," and the classic "Virginia Beach Be Da Bomb!"), then this be da vacation spot for you.

—*Michael Tully*

Virginia Beach is sort of like Seaside Heights, New Jersey—or, Sleazeside, as locals call it—but without good pizza. It's kind of stuck in a tough position, because if you are looking for an amusement park kind of vacation (and are from the mid-Atlantic area), you typically go to Ocean City, Maryland. If you want someplace beautiful and relaxing, you go to the Outer Banks in North Carolina. If you're looking for golf, you go to Myrtle Beach, South Carolina. If you're looking to party, you go to Dewey Beach, Delaware. Virginia Beach isn't really known for anything. When I was at the University of Richmond, our Beach Week always took place in the Outer Banks of North Carolina. We never even entertained the idea of going to any beach in Virginia.

—*Chris Naughton*

Virginia Beach is a miserable crap-hole, particularly during winter. The ocean wind howls continually, reducing your testicles to shriveled raisins. . . . Once summer hits, Virginia Beach awakens from its slumber and returns to the land of the living. . . . There's nothing special about Virginia Beach; it's a resort community that overgrew its capabilities and hasn't figured out how to clean up its garbage. For a quick vacation in July or August, Virginia Beach can be quite a bit of fun. Anything beyond that— or during a nonsummer month—is a miserable, mind-numbing experience.

—Last Story *magazine*

Virginia Beach sucks. That's all there is to it.

—*Neil*

PERFECTLY ILLUSTRATIVE HEADLINES FROM *THE VIRGINIAN-PILOT*

- "Man With Assault Rifle Robs Brinks Employee in Virginia Beach"
- "Beach Man Pleads Guilty to Killing Mother, Stuffing Her in Freezer"
- "Former Go-Go Dancer Helps Students Shape Up with Sexy Moves"
- "Search for Driver Who Jumped Off Bay Bridge-Tunnel Called Off"

The supposedly desirable neighborhood of Columbia Heights.

Washington, DC

Justice to All

Population: 572,059
Unemployment: 6.8%
Median Household Income: $40,127
Violent Crime Rate: 1627.7
Climate: Conservative, uptight, poorly dressed, and humid
Average "Jumbo" Pizza Slice Width: Eleven inedible inches

Ideal for: POTUS, Federal Employees, Interns, Crack Addicts/Mayors, Yuppies, Undergrads, Young Ambitious Politicos, Older Established Politicos, Lawyer Types, Lobbyists, Meathead Idiots, Smokers, Arsonists

Cultural Highlights: Go-go Music/Shootings, Arson, Glad Handing Suit-and-tie Mixers on the Hill, Carjacking, Crack, Antigentrification/Sophomoric Graffiti, Urban Sprawl, Humidity, Drum Circles, BORF, Urine

As America's only city-state and the seat of its democracy, Washington, D.C. is at least uniquely terrible. In its defense, the National Mall, flanked on all sides by the Smithsonian and assorted symbols of American majesty, is lovely and provides hours of entertainment for visitors, most of whom appear to be either school-children or European. The White House seems a bit small in person, and good luck finding a cup of coffee from anywhere other than Starbucks, but all in all D.C.'s not the worst place in the world to spend a weekend. (That would be Des Moines, Iowa.)

The problem is that outside of the designated tourist area, Washington, D.C. is nothing more than a sprawling, crime-ridden ghetto (with the exception of yuppie-approved safe zones like Georgetown and Alexandria,

Virginia). To drive through greater Washington (the woefully inefficient subway and price-gouging cabbies make owning an automobile something of a necessity) is to traverse a landscape of shuttered buildings, vacant lots, Mexican day laborer depots, swampland, housing projects, and nonpotable water. One wonders, while traipsing about the city, why the British couldn't have burned more stuff.

Unless you happen to be the president-elect of the United States, relocating to Washington, D.C. should remain an option left largely unexplored.

Quotes

My hatred for D.C. is in full flower, much like the overrated cherry blossoms.
>   —*Ben Ikenson, author,* The Daredevil's Manual
>   *and* Patents: Ingenious Inventions

D.C. is great to visit, but if you have to live anywhere near, the only places are Fairfax and old towne Alexandria. Anywhere else and you are living in a slum pretending you are making life better for the shitheads who will eventually rob you.
>   —*Alan Stanwick*

No one here has the slightest idea of how to operate any sort of vehicle. They cannot operate a turn signal, do not understand the concept of remaining in their own lane, and incessantly switch lanes in search of an ever faster moving lane which does not exist. Also, nothing is cheap. Real estate prices are seriously inflated. Rent is sky-high and none of the residences are worth even half of what people are paying. Yes, the museums are free, but factor in the entirely aggravating experience of trying to learn anything surrounded by screaming, uncontrolled children and even free is too expensive. And let's not forget the drinking water: I think floating dead bodies are a common occurrence in the Potomac River, which, yes, does supply our water. What a lovely idea. Does my Brita filter do much to battle the impending doom I feel every time I take a drink? Not really.

—*Summer James*

AUTHOR'S VIEW

You have not truly encountered rudeness until you've shopped for groceries at the Whole Foods on P Street in Washington, D.C., where entitlement and progressive dietary requirements conspire to create a landscape of uppity Caucasians stocking their carts full of free-range chicken and pinot noir with the unswerving determination of great white sharks in a sea full of blood. All elements of polite society are thrown to the wayside like so much white bread as wave after wave of upwardly mobile gentrifiers race to their Volkswagens in a panic, intent on arriving safely home to their brownstones before nightfall.

→ **A DISSENTING OPINION**

D.C. has so many cultural opportunities . . . and most of them are free! There are great restaurants, including any kind of ethnic food you could ask for, and tons of bars. Within a twenty-minute drive is hiking (Great Falls, Virginia), or right in the city you can spend a day relaxing along the river. You can live in an apartment that isn't the size of a closet and even have outdoor space . . . and you can afford it! Or, once you're older, you can live in an actual house with a yard right in the middle of the city! The subway system is clean. Really clean. Georgetown on a nice spring day . . . sigh! There are also great running/biking trails throughout the city and the suburbs, so you don't have to risk your life on the streets.

—Jackie Endriss

Well . . . at least there's electricity.

Yuba City, CA

Population: 36,758
Unemployment: 8%
Median Household Income: $32,858
Violent Crime Rate: 534.7
Local Arsonists' Preferred Target: The Islamic Center of Yuba City
Sister Armpit: Marysville, CA
Ideal for: Fundamentalist Rednecks, Fruit Tramps, Lo Ball Poker Dealers, Sikhs, The Unemployed, Ex-cons, Hispanics
Cultural Highlights: "Rand McNally 329 and I Love It" T-shirts, The Town Pump, Lo Ball Poker Palace, The

America's a really big place. To be the very worst takes determination, hard work, imagination, and a certain flair for catastrophe. The competition is fierce. Camden, New Jersey, isn't gonna just up and gentrify. And no one's gonna slap a coat of paint on Detroit or infuse D.C. with a couple of decent restaurants anytime soon. To win this thing, you've gotta want it. Want it real bad. Anywhere can suck, just ask most of Ohio. We're talking about the worst place to live in the *entire* country. So, whatta ya got? A devastated economy? Rampant violent crime? A Starbucks littering every corner? Inedible pizza? No subway? Please.

This is a singular achievement, the culmination of decades of hard work and a lengthy and complicated application process. To receive this designation is to forever function as a symbol of despair, as a harbinger for future towns slipping slowly into ruin. Year after year, Yuba City, California, defies the odds, consistently finishing at or near the very bottom of virtually each and every national poll. How do they do it? Only the locals know. Sure, they've got some impressive help from the neighboring abomination known as Marysville, but still . . . it's quite a feat.

Quotes

I would like to nominate Yuba City–Marysville, California, my hometown, as being the very worst in America. It has been at the bottom or near the bottom of the *Rand McNally* index for over thirty years. Here are some quick facts:

- The town was destroyed in the Flood of 1955, then evacuated in 1987 and 1999 due to more flooding.
- Yuba City was home to Juan Corona, who murdered twenty-five people in six weeks in 1971, making him the worst serial killer in U.S. history to that point.
- The town fathers once sued *Time* magazine for calling it a "pestilential, mosquito-laden wasteland," among other things.
- The town also once staged a public burning of *Rand McNally*.
- The area boasts a startling unemployment rate, depending upon the season.
- We've got one of the highest juvenile delinquency rates in California, too.
- It's 115 degrees in the summer, then gets socked by a solid month of fog during the winter.
- The poverty and education levels are comparable to those of Mississippi.
- It's the reddest county in California (63 percent voted for Bush).

Also, it's virtually impossible to escape, thanks to the fact that there are no freeways around Yuba City. To get out, you have to drive thirty miles on two-lane country roads, which can be so dangerous during the winter (thanks to the fog), that it's necessary to have a police car escort you for the first twenty or thirty miles. It takes three or four hours to get to San Francisco, which is only about 120 miles away.

—*Janet Ilaqua*

I really can't stand Yuba. My father and brother live there and I'm constantly reminding them of how run down it is. When my brother was in the Air Force, he was told that the state prison gives released prisoners a one-way bus ticket and the farthest it will take them is Yuba City. So that's where most of the ex-cons end up.

—*Anonymous*

PERFECTLY ILLUSTRATIVE HEADLINES FROM THE *APPEAL-DEMOCRAT*

- "Body in River Surfaces"
- "What's in the Water up There?"
- "A Night to Take Back the Streets"

The Republic teeters in Bismarck, ND.

Dishonorable Mention Appendix

The breadth and scope of America's worst towns is truly something to behold. Here are a few that just barely missed the cut, despite trying really, really hard.

Ankeny, IA

Ankeny is an ugly, pretentious little town . . . with marshy pond areas near the edge of town that double as huge mosquito breeding grounds. During the hot, humid summers, you have to run from your car to your house if you don't want to be sucked dry by a black cloud of hungry skeeters.

—*DeAnn Rossetti*

Bend, OR

Bend is where beauty goes to die. There is nothing attractive about the town, not even in the "cool artsy derelict" sort of way. It's as attractive as a strip mall, as a low-budget subdivision, as a fast-food bathroom. It is just plain ugly.

—*Anonymous*

Boca Raton, FL

By far and away the worst American town has to be Boca Raton, Florida . . . I cringe whenever I drive past or, God forbid, visit. It is the e-mail-spamming capital of the world, and the Gambino crime family apparently has an outpost there as well. It is an odd collection of retirees and "entrepreneurs." By entrepreneur, I mean scumbag scammers. Boca Raton looks like all the suburbs/exurbs of America, filled with foreign cars, Bed Bath & Beyonds, and gated communities. The people exhibit accents from Long Island and New Jersey, gold chains and nugget pinky rings, and of course huge fake tits. It is a place with no redeeming value whatsoever.

—*Sheraz Sharif*

Boring, OR

What sucks about living in Boring is any time people ask for your address over the phone and you say "Boring, Oregon," *every time* they respond, "Is it really boring in Boring, Oregon?" It drove me nuts.

—*Amy Hodgin*

Bozeman, MT

Used to be a small agricultural community, surrounded by open space, farms, and ranches. Then they kicked those people out to make room for subdivisions, strip malls, and SUVs. They've squandered their once beautiful environment and turned it into Anytown, USA. It's so disgusting, it might be off the scales of the crap-o-meter.

—*Justin Disney*

Cambridge, MA

One of the most arrogant, intellectually snobbish places on earth.

—*Anonymous*

Cerrillos, NM

So close to civilization, yet so far away. Aside from no garbage pick up, no mail delivery, and having to carry water to your dwelling from tanks provided by the National Guard, the village is a collection of self-built hovels or crumbling adobes and mine shacks from the 1880s. It's a ghost town where people still live. There is one store which seems to be open, but it's full of nothing but dusty crap.

—*B. Erisman*

Coos Bay, OR

It is on the beautiful Oregon coast, but has no tourist facilities other than an Indian Casino built inside an old saw mill. No beach resorts, decent restaurants, or anything nice. A real scrubby rundown little town completely out of place in a beautiful region of the Pacific Northwest.

—*Greg Colman*

Cortez, CO

I almost got ass raped while waiting at a bus stop. A friend and I were waiting to transfer to a Greyhound bus to take us to Yellowstone Park. It was late, around midnight, and this old lady came by, staring at us with terror in her eyes. She warned us that the bars were about to close, and we had better find indoor shelter immediately, before the drunk guys hit the streets.

—*Adam Mutterperl*

Des Moines, IA

I tried to order pizza from a downtown "eatery" and asked for two slices of cheese. They sent me two pieces of Kraft singles. Then, when I explained what I wanted, they served Elio's. I should have stuck with the Kraft singles.

—*Chris Naughton*

Douglasville, GA

It's a real shithole that might as well be called Hee-Haw Town, USA. Douglasville has always been a simple, slow-paced place for rednecks and hillbillies to while away their useless lives spotlight huntin', muddin', cow tippin', and gatherin' with the rest of the cultural elite at Waffle House.

—*Rick Pace*

Dundalk, MD

This offshoot town of Baltimore city is a White Trash Ghetto at its most terrifying. Shirtless four-year-old children stomp down the sidewalks with the authority of a hardened criminal.

—*Michael Tully*

East St. Louis, MO

I got lost there and while driving under an overpass, saw graffiti that said "Kill the white Man." It's basically the same as Granite City, Illinois, but with black people who aren't as apathetic about their situation and seem to have goals, even if it is killing the white man.

—*Beth Dowell*

Fall River, MA

Home of the Dollar Stores and Kmart, where anything over ten bucks is way too much and owning a souped-up Toyota Celica is as cool as it comes. All the houses are lower middle class/working class, and because many of them are owned by proud Portuguese immigrants, you get all these over-the-top, ridiculous attempts at poshness. I draw your attention to the gilded lion statues at the gate, or the fake classical column-portico on the "faux" front door (that's an utterly *fake* front door—the real entrance is around the back!!). Most locals have never set foot outside a fifteen-mile radius of their homes.

—*Nancy Barbosa*

Forks, WA

Ramshackle bars are packed with chain-smoking, owl-hating rednecks who nail down vests to tree trunks as warnings against environmentalists. The big Thriftway supermarket and bowling alley serve as the main recreational venues, aside from extracurricular wife-beating or pounding the local Makah Indians who wander into town. It's a festering wound of a town plagued with chronic unemployment, alcoholism, and drug abuse. But . . . the fishing ain't half bad.

—*Gabby Hyman*

Groton, CT

It's *very* New Englandy—meaning if your great-great grandparents and everyone after them didn't live here their entire lives, then you are an outsider and shall be damned for all eternity. The town is dirty, dry, washed-up, and boring.

—*Stephanie Wolfe*

Hinesville, GA

The sort of town that everyone talks about moving away from. It's an endless topic—escaping to wherever there are better jobs, less dust that seems to settle in your mouth, or more shady trees to shield you from the sun. I never figured out if it was just a rumor that the alligators near our backyard regularly gobbled up neighborhood cats.

—*Roberta Beach Jacobson*

Indianapolis, IN

Smells like a sewer backup.

—*Kyle Bernstein*

Interior, SD

It festers on the dirt floor of a basin surrounded by the dirt hills of the Badlands. It is small and sparsely popu-lated, but spread out, sort of a trailer park with a main street. The single greatest impression I took away with me was the stench of rotting meat, which is thick and permeating. Within a few minutes of entering town, I was swarmed by house flies, which, coupled with the dry heat and the pungent smell of carrion, made the short visit even shorter. This town is the epitome of squalor.

—*Gwydion M. Hastur*

Kalona, IA

Kalona is an ugly little town that smells like a rancid sausage.

—*DeAnn Rossetti*

Kissimmee, FL

The redheaded stepchild of Orlando. Not quite the reason to come to Florida, but right next door. This is a town that advertises it's okay to be the neighbor to a great thing. Like Canada is going to have their chamber of commerce advertise "Come to Canada, where you are not in the United States, but almost." Seriously, they proclaim themselves "The neighbor to Orlando." Kissimmee is Orlando's bitch.

—*Mike Miller*

Los Angeles, CA

A city big enough to be a real cultural mecca, yet is sadly a mecca of all the worst culture in America: television, fake tits, smog, and an obsession with the automobile.

—*Scott Moe*

Lynn, MA

No list of true shitholes would be complete without the town of Lynn, a toxic dump ten miles north of Boston. It is the home of nothing but assholes, most without dental plans. Lynn, Lynn the City of Sin, you never come out the way you went in.

—*Blammy*

Memphis, TN

The grossest bathroom I've ever been in was at a gas station in Memphis where the sink was full of greenish thick fluid.

—*Anne*

Oklahoma City, OK

I am convinced that the Trail of Tears didn't get its name until they stopped in Oklahoma and were told this was their new home. The place is completely flat and green foliage must have been outlawed because everything is brown, drab, and boring.

—*Alan Stanwick*

Palo Alto, CA

Smart people, nice weather, lots of money . . . so why is it the most boring place on earth?

—*Scott Moe*

Peoria, IL

Peoria is the least fit town in the country. On an average day, you'll see one—maybe two—people who are not suffering from severe obesity. The people of Peoria are so overweight, movie theater seats have been made six inches wider. I spent one evening at the West Peoria Bar and Grill and couldn't sit in the bar for more than three minutes at a time because the cigarette smoke was so thick it made your eyes water and your lungs burn. These people are the biggest group of hicks, who are entertained by NASCAR while indulging in vast quantities of greasy fast foods and Miller High Life.

—*Daniel Boniface*

Quilcene, WA

Quilcene is a sorry semirural collection of gas stations, run-down double-wide trailers, crack houses, and stoned teenagers.

—*Douglas Gantenbein*

Rochester, NY

I have lived in Rochester for the last four years and I can only liken it to unrelenting abysmal torment. Most people below the age of thirty-five refer to the town as "Crapchester." It sits on Lake Ontario, which once caught fire from the pollution in it, and the air must contain an obscene amount of carcinogens. The sky is usually gray, we only get something like seventy clear days a year, and last winter it snowed for twenty-nine straight days in January.

—*William Owen*

Rolla, MO

A gloomy, unimpressive college town, Rolla boasts famed speed traps and crummy, outdated steakhouse-type restaurants that smell like day-old ashtrays. My husband once accidentally ingested a live bug from the salad bar at one such dive. He gagged and then looked through his lettuce to find the bug's sidekick. The manager, full of Rolla class, did not even offer a refund.

—*Lori Erickson Trump*

Trona, CA

Trona is a town out in the middle of the desert in California, near Death Valley. It is the site of a former borax mine and currently plays host to a number of burnt-out trailer parks. There are also several old chemical companies there (now defunct). Because of the heavy chemical activity, the soil itself has turned a number of disturbing colors, and there are sinkholes aplenty.

—*Charlene Butterfield*

Vancouver, WA

It's a run-down methamphetamine junkie haven, an industrial shitpile with depressed peeps and awful weather located in the middle of some of the most astonishingly gorgeous geography on earth.

—*Meghan Sutherland*

Wilkes-Barre, PA

You can get the true sense of the area and its loser people by watching *The Deer Hunter*. This was the reason Christopher Walken wanted to blow his brains out, not because he was tortured in Vietnam. As you drive up Route 81 into this area, you descend into a valley of despair. It also happens to be a favorite burying place for the Mafia.

—*Greg DeCicco*

Yonkers, NY

Yonkers is the car theft capital of Westchester County. High taxes, racism, and Guidos abound . . . what more could you want?

—*Chris Cotter*

Acknowledgments

Thank you to everyone who contributed to this project. I am particularly indebted to Beth Dowell, Lindsey Duvall, Alan Stanwick, Andrew Buckley, Jeff Biener, Mary Meriam, Angela Ambrosini-Haliski, Daniel Greenberg, and Sean Desmond.